ETHICS

ETHICS

A Lawyer's Perspective with Case Studies

Dr. Orscini L. Beard

iUniverse

ETHICS
A LAWYER'S PERSPECTIVE WITH CASE STUDIES

iUniverse books may be ordered through booksellers or by contacting:

iUniverse
1663 Liberty Drive
Bloomington, IN 47403
www.iuniverse.com
844-349-9409

ISBN: 978-1-6632-3328-8 (sc)
ISBN: 978-1-6632-3329-5 (e)

Library of Congress Control Number: 2022909194

Print information available on the last page.

iUniverse rev. date: 06/20/2022

This book is dedicated to all of the people raised in Delray, Michigan; to my late brothers, Ronald M. Nicholson, Lester Earl Beard, and Tyrone Beard, whose loved and devotion to the family will never be forgotten; to my late mother, Leola V. Mayes, for her love; to my wife, Bertha M. Beard, who is what Jehovah God has given to me to help me along the way; and, of course, to my children, who are my inspiration. They are what I am.

CONTENTS

PREFACE

The purpose of this book is to assist aspiring young attorneys, law students, and future lawyers in avoiding the pitfalls of everyday practice. Attorneys encounter many challenging situations, many of which could have been very devastating; some were devastating. Accordingly, this book has been written to serve as an analysis of the most commonly made mistakes in the legal profession and presents clear explanations of how to correct them. It has also been prepared as a reference work for the general practitioner of criminal law, who may want to check questionable issues in criminal matters. Therefore, the book can be used either as a supplement or as a handbook as individual circumstances may decree.

As one peruses this book, he or she may ask, "What right does this person have to tell me how to practice criminal law when he made a mess of it?" The answer is simple. Most lawyers are unwilling to tell the raw, naked truth of their trials and tribulations. Preferably, as experienced lawyers, they present the upside of the practice of law with little or no emphasis on the downside of it, which is currently being observed by the most competent and carefully disciplined attorneys.

Thus, the writer says to this reader, "Here are the principles of professional responsibility, which are necessary for an acceptable practice in the legal profession." From the above discussion, one can readily see that we all have this concept of right and wrong. It has been embedded in us since our inception by our parents, churches, and schools. Indeed, the terms must be equated with what is morally right or wrong. That is, the terms must be construed to mean legally right or wrong in the everyday practice of those persons whose very existence depends on making the correct choices or decisions in order to merit the respect of their colleagues.

After reflecting on this explanation of what is morally or legally correct, one must recognize another fundamental fact: Some questions cannot be settled unequivocally in terms of "right" or "wrong." The reasons are quite clear. In some instances, lawyers differ in their observations of some given practices. In other instances, lawyers find in practice what was once widely endorsed is now disappearing, for example, the subtle distinction between what is considered right and wrong. In still other instances, the disciplinary counsels find situations that lie beyond any detailed analysis, such as the line between acceptable standards. As a result, no reputable lawyer dare proclaims final rulings on many practices.

However, even though the correct way to practice, in a sense, is an arbitrary and sometimes unsettled matter, specific standards do exist, and the careful practitioner must abide by them. These are standards upon which this author bases his compilation of these mistakes in the legal profession.

To master the standards of legal responsibility, one should begin with the realization that he or she is engaging in a fascinating field. From the first lesson, one learns the central principle of conduct: how to practice within the challenging standards of this exciting profession.

ACKNOWLEDGMENTS

I want to give thanks to Jehovah God, through him in whom all things are possible. His guidance and blessing were with me every step of the way. When problems seemed overwhelming, he was there to strengthen me and place people in my path to assist in this endeavor. I am grateful to my wife for her understanding, patience, and continual support in pursuing this book, and for my children (Orscini, II, Tafari, Tarik, and Takiyah) and my many grandchildren. Finally, I am incredibly grateful to my daughter-in-law, Myiesha Beard, for her assistance and guidance in completing this book.

INTRODUCTION

On the twenty-first day of April 1983, I received the results from my bar exam. One day after the federal government declared the city of Baton Rouge to be in a state of emergency. I was sworn in as a member of the Louisiana Bar on the twenty-seventh day of April 1983. Shortly after that, I entered the private practice of law with the law firm of Johnson, Ritzie, Thomas, and Taylor on 72nd Avenue in Baton Rouge, Louisiana.

I was interested in pursuing a career in taxation, especially since I had just finished attending Emory University Law School's taxation program. If someone would have told me that criminal law would be the essence of my practice, I would have laughed. The practice of criminal law was not on my agenda.

I initially received a few cases concerning tax issues, but they were not enough to sustain a living for my family. So I had to supplement my income with other civil matters, including divorce cases, successions, and corporation matters. Attorney fees derived from these cases were sufficient for my livelihood, and in a matter of months, I was able to save a substantial down payment for a new house. We resided with my in-laws for two years and then moved into a new home located on Buttonwood Street in the Glen Oaks subdivision.

My practice was doing well for an inexperienced lawyer of four months. Again, I saved a substantial amount of money from legal fees, but my tax practice was not flourishing as I had hoped. So I continued to practice civil law until a prospective client walked into the office and asked, "Can anyone here handle a criminal matter?" The client waved a cashier's check for five thousand dollars for any takers. Ernest and the other lawyers declined the invitation. Then Ernest asked me, "Would you want to handle a criminal case?"

This was not a difficult decision. "Hell, with $5,000 in hand, how difficult can it be to defend a client in a criminal matter!"

As we talked about the facts of the case, I envisioned how I would defend him. Having little or no knowledge of criminal matters, I thought it best to spend time studying. I read several articles and books on the subject. They were of significant impact, not so much as to the case at bar, but on how I would defend future criminal cases. Still, I searched for a topic that would give me some insight into how to handle plea-bargaining. Deep down inside, I was not ready to take on the responsibility or burden of trying a criminal case, although subconsciously, I knew that going to trial was a remote possibility. I tried to negotiate a plea bargain, but the assistant district attorney, Joe Lockwitt, did not offer any deals. My client had to plead to the charges as billed by the district attorney's office. Vince Wilkinson of the public defender's office represented the other defendant involved in this case. Since there were no acceptable pleas in the case, we were compelled to try the case before Honorable Judge Doug Moreau.

The judge called our case for trial. I wore a blue suit, white shirt, and a maroon tie adorned with white polka dots for the trial. I felt extraordinarily sharp and ready for the occasion. Of course, I do not have to tell you how nervous I was. I had never tried a case before a judge and explained this to my co-counsel. He told me, "Follow my lead, and you will be fine." I followed his instructions to the letter and pretended to know what I was doing in the trial. After Vince finished cross-examining the state's first witness, it was my turn to cross-examine the witness. Admittedly, I knew what I was doing after Vince's eloquent cross-examination. Then without any warning, Judge Moreau interrupted my examination of the witness. While I was asking some very pertinent questions, he decided to cross-examine the witness himself. For a moment, I entertained these questions, until I felt he was taking over my case and confusing the issues. At that point, I scolded the judge, telling him, "Please allow me to try my own case." He acquiesced. The cross-examinations of the state's other witnesses were becoming very exciting, and I looked forward to the challenge.

Then the state rested its case. It was the defense's turn to present our case, and I was ready to seize the moment. We called our first witness. I took the lead by trying to contradict the testimony of the police officers and the other witnesses. It proved to be extremely beneficial, or so I thought. We rested our case. I gave my first summation, which I thought was very eloquent and poetic. As this was a bench, not a jury trial, the judge determined the verdict. He ruled in the state's favor but rescinded his initial judgment of incarceration by giving both defendants one day in the parish prison.

As I was leaving the courthouse, Vince stopped me and said, "If you do not practice criminal law, it will be one of the greatest disgraces in the history of the legal profession." His statement only supplemented what I already knew: I was meant to practice criminal law.

> Should an attorney allow a judge to cross-examine witnesses to the extent he or she becomes the trial lawyer? If so, to what degree? What ethical consideration is jeopardized when an attorney does not address an overzealous judge in cross-examining witnesses?

CHAPTER 1

My First Jury Trial

Most criminal lawyers or criminal justice students understand that there are two types of trials in the United States. First, all citizens have a right to an impartial jury trial guaranteed by the Sixth Amendment. If a citizen elects not to utilize the jury trial process, there is the option of selecting a bench trial, when the issue is more technical. A jury trial for a first-year attorney is extremely rare, and more often than not, a first-year attorney seeks the guidance of a seasoned attorney before attempting to try a case before a jury.

When I returned to the office, my coworkers asked, "How did you do?" to which I responded, "I like trying criminal cases and would like to increase my skills in that area." It was not long before another client came into the office, asking for someone to represent him. Again, he had a considerable amount of money for attorney's fees. I was eager to improve my knowledge of criminal law, so we discussed the merits of his case and an affirmative defense. Shortly after that, I filed the necessary motions.

The first assistant district attorney, Barry Wilkinson, offered a minimum sentence. But because my client was a second offender, he could not receive probation. My client declined the offer, and as a result, I had no choice but to try the case. The difference in this case from the first trial before a judge was that my client, Larry Paul, was exposed to ten possible years of incarceration with the Department of Safety and Corrections. Here, the honorable Barry Marioneaux informed me, "If you try this case, and the defendant is convicted, he will be given a ten-year sentence; if you plead him, he will receive five years."

Again, I was caught off balance because I thought this case would be tried months later. But I was wrong, as usual. I had read many books concerning preparation for trial and preparing a trial notebook. The books had information on how to select a jury during voir dire and to define an opening statement. The jury selection was going quite well, but the pressure of trying my first jury trial, coupled with the fact that my client could be incarcerated for ten years, was taking its toll. It took several hours to sit a jury of six persons.

Opening statements were presented within the prescribed time allotted by the judge. The state called its first witness. On cross-examination, I contradicted some of the witnesses, but the critical witnesses were unraveled by my trial techniques. My defense was straightforward. Yes, he was there, but his intent was clearly to use the money for more alcohol. In essence, he was an alcoholic. On direct, I was able to use the testimony of an expert in substance abuse and the officer who arrested him while he was breaking into the machines at the laundromat to our advantage. On the one hand, the expert explained that being an alcoholic is considered a disease. The officer explained the arrest; that is, my client was extremely intoxicated. Thus, my client's inability to discern between right and wrong became an affirmative defense to the crime. Both sides rested. I thought my summation was perfect, but I was worried about the jury. The jury returned a responsive verdict, and everyone was pleased.

After the trial, I informed both the assistant district attorney and Judge Marioqoeaux that I was impressed with their courtroom decorum and that I learned a lot from them. I also mentioned that this was my first jury trial. They were shocked. Of course, it pleased me very much, given the extent of district attorney's legal reputation. Interestingly, my client was never sentenced or incarcerated for the crime. Until this day, he continues to walk the streets of Port Allen without serving one day for the crime. The assistant district attorney and the judge are as much aware of this fact as I am.

> Should criminal defendants be given higher sentences because they choose to avail themselves of their constitutional right to a jury trial?
>
> What ethical consideration is involved when a judge indicates that he or she will increase

the sentence if the defendant avails himself or herself of a trial instead of pleading?

Moreover, what duty, if any, does the assistant district attorney, judge, or defense attorney have to enforce the verdict of conviction in this matter?

CHAPTER 2

The Pleas

Most successful criminal prosecutions in the United States—85 to 95 percent—end not with jury trials but with plea bargains. Plea bargains are agreements between defendants and prosecutors in which defendants agree to plead guilty to some or all of the charges against them in exchange for concessions from the prosecutors. These agreements allow prosecutors to focus their time and resources on other cases, and reduce the number of trials judges need to oversee.

State of Louisiana
Versus
Glen Marshall

This case involves organized crime. Glen Marshall and four other defendants were responsible for stealing more than a half-million dollars from Baton Rouge banks. They also stole more than a million dollars from banks in New Orleans before coming to Baton Rouge. A month before that, they embezzled more than a million dollars from Jackson, Mississippi, banks. The money financed their drug operation in Oakland, California.

The process used in obtaining the ill-gotten funds was straightforward. An individual interceded and inspected bank statements from viable businesses in a particular area. They would then send a professional thief to burglarize those businesses whose bank statements revealed a positive balance. This person stole checks from either the middle or the back of the checkbook and deliver them checks to the clients.

Interestingly, the burglar would disappear from the city after delivering the checks. His involvement in the scheme was limited only to his expertise. His "clients" would fill out the blank checks and deposit them in different banks in the Baton Rouge area. Once the checks ran their proper course, the clients sent a mule to withdraw the money. They would maintain a modest balance in order to not draw attention to themselves or the account. The mule would generally be a professional white person. In most instances, a white female was used in carrying out the scheme.

The banks reported the thefts to local authorities, so law enforcement agencies were able to notify other banks who were not victims of the scheme. On the day in question, two professional mules walked into the Bank of Baton Rouge to withdraw monies from their bogus saving or checking account. The teller was very suspicious of these persons after being warned the bank could be the next target for the robbers. She notified her supervisor as she pretended to seek approval for the transaction. The supervisor, in turn, called the authorities. Sergeant John Webber arrived within minutes of the call and began to watch the activities of the thieves. One of the mules sensed that detectives were watching her and began to act nervously. After completing the transaction, the detectives followed the two people, who were arrested for forgery and felony theft.

After being interviewed by the forgery division, the mule implicated the clients. However, the detectives did not have a clue as to their whereabouts. To catch them, Sergeant Webber of the East Baton Rouge Sheriff's Department, Forgery Division, contacted all the bonding agencies in Baton Rouge, telling them, "If anyone tries to bond these young ladies out, please notify me." To this end, the clients went to the A-1 Bonding Company to secure the women's freedom from jail. They left the name of the motel where they were staying and the telephone number for the agent to contact them once the young women were released.

The sheriff's department arrested the clients at the motel on 102 counts of forgery and 78 counts of felony theft. Glen, one of the clients, called from the parish prison for Ernest Johnson because he had heard of his reputation in defending indigents. Since Ernest did not practice criminal law, he referred the case to others in the firm.

The next day, the five defendants were interviewed. One of the defendants wanted a white attorney because of the adage that white attorneys can better deal with the legal system than black attorneys. Initially, they were sort of apprehensive about hiring the firm because of its inexperience in criminal matters. Nevertheless, they continued to request visits from a member of the firm. I brought contraband to them, such as cigarettes and personal hygiene items. I continued to work for weeks without the retainer fee by the defendants. Eventually, Glen said, "We want to retain your services. How much?" I responded by requesting a fee of $10,000 each. He said, "Let me make a few calls." The next day, I was contacted by someone who identified herself as a member of the Marshall family from Oakland, California. She indicated that she would be arriving in Baton Rouge the next day and asked if I could arrange to meet her.

At our meeting, I learned she was Glen's wife. We discussed the fee and representation of her husband. She needed to talk with him before retaining the firm. After visiting him, she made a few calls from the office. Shortly after, I received a call from Glen's brother, who informed me, "Western Union will transmit your retainer fee before the business day. You will receive the sum of $5,000 every other day from various members of the Marshall family until the $40,000 was paid." I received the entire fee within the time prescribed.

We began to prepare our defense by filing all the necessary motions. Since Glen had been incarcerated for more than sixty days, I filed a 701 motion. It allows any incarcerated person who has not been billed or indicted by the district attorney's office within sixty days of arrest to be released from his or her bond obligation or released from prison. The judge and district attorney's office were determined not to release them from their bond obligation. Consequently, in open court, Assistant District Attorney Joe Lotwitt filed a bill of information on the charges after seventy-six days had elapsed, along with a request for a handwriting sample from all the defendants.

Accordingly, the court ordered them to submit to handwriting analysis. The defendants supplied the court with copies of their handwriting, but the experts were unable to associate their handwriting samples with those of the checks deposited for collection at the various banks in Baton Rouge. Glen could pick up a check with two fingers and write on the check without leaving any fingerprints. The district attorney's office was baffled. The only evidence that connected the clients to the crime was the testimony of the white women. Glen Marshall, who was labeled the leader, was using a fictitious name. The authorities in Littleton, Colorado, wanted him for forgery and felony theft.

A few months before coming to Louisiana, Marshall had absconded from a jury trial. The court tried him in absentia and convicted for the crimes charged. Moreover, Glen had been recently released from federal prison, where he was serving a sentence for forgery and felony theft. Joe, who was prosecuting the case, did not know this. One of the codefendants, who was represented by Alex Walls Jr., entered a plea with the district attorney's office for five years with credit for time served. He had already completed one year in the parish prison.

Having this information and knowing that time was of the essence in terms of his fugitive status and prior criminal convictions, Glen also agreed to a plea bargain with Joe. He and the other defendants received a sentence of eighteen months; Glen's brother received eight months. All were released immediately except Glen because his fingerprints revealed that he was not John Marshall, the name he had been using; he was Glen Marshall. He did not fight extradition to Colorado. I also defended him in Colorado. He received a sentence of five years.

After I returned from Colorado, one of the codefendants, who was still serving his Louisiana sentence, contacted me by telephone to discuss the possibility of having his five-year sentence reduced. I did not receive a telephone call from a member of his immediate family requesting the services. I went to the parish prison to discuss the feasibility of having his sentence reduced and my retainer fee. He indicated he had to make a few calls. The next day, I received a call from his sister or mother (I don't remember from whom, but at any rate, a call was made to my office), requesting that I contact them. I contacted the mother and discussed the particulars but not the facts of the case. She wired the retainer fee by Western Union of $5,000.

Before the filing of the motion for a reduction in sentence, I discussed with the honorable Joseph Keogh the possibility of reducing the defendant's sentence, especially since his sentence was twice as high as the other defendants' sentences. I pointed out that the client was not the mastermind of the scheme but only a participant. The judge told me to file the motion. I filed an ex parte motion for a sentence reduction and a judgment of release. An ex parte motion or discussion occurs when the defense attorney or prosecuting attorney discusses the case with the judge when the other attorney is not present.

He commuted the sentence to eighteen months. The defendant was eligible for immediate release. A week later, Joe asked me about the ex parte motion. I explained the nature of the motion to him, which he felt should not have been signed without notice to the district attorney's office, mainly since the judge was without jurisdiction. Because fifty-four days had elapsed, the judge could not correct his sentence. By then, the defendant had been released and was on his way back to California.

> The ethical consideration: Should a defense attorney who is aware that his or her client has pending charges, convictions, and is involved in other criminal activities reveal this information to the proper authorities before entering a plea bargaining?

If so, to what extent should this information be revealed?

There are other ethical considerations in this case. First, is it proper to introduce contraband into a parish prison?

Second, should an attorney interview a client without receiving a call or being contacted by a member of the family?

Third, should an attorney receive a retainer from an organized crime group? And if so, should the fee be declared by reporting the same to federal authorities since the amount sent was done in order to circumvent the $10,000 reporting act?

Finally, should an attorney contact a client before the previous attorney is released?

Is it improper to discuss a case with a member of the client's family?

Should the attorney be contacted by a member of the client's family prior to visiting him of her in prison?

Should an attorney have an ex parte discussion with the judge without a representative from the district attorney's office present?

Should any ex parte motions be filed without notice to the district attorney's office?

If an attorney is aware of the fifty-four-day period, should he or she divulge this information to the judge prior to having the judgment signed?

Should an attorney represent a defendant whose defense is antagonistic to the other defendant(s)?

CHAPTER 3

The First-Degree Murder Trial

Capital murder is used interchangeably with first-degree murder. This involves a murder that subjects the defendant to the death penalty provision of a state criminal code. For this to apply, the defendant must have violated one or more of the subtitles to the statute of capital murder. This is to say that he or she committed some horrific extenuating circumstance, often called "special circumstance," in addition to causing the death. This may include such things as murdering a police officer, murdering a child or anyone over the age of sixty-five, or murdering multiple victims. To explore this concept, consider the following capital murder definition in Louisiana Revised Statute 14:14:30: "First Degree Murder. Generally, an attorney must have practiced for at least five (5) years in order to be appointed to a Capital murder cases."

The Commonwealth of Virgina
Versus
Angelo Congo

I received a call from Angelo Congo, who was incarcerated in the East Baton Rouge Parish Prison, requesting my services. I did not receive a call from his immediate family. I went to the prison to discuss his case. He informed me that he was charged with the crime of first-degree murder in Norfolk, Virginia. After several discussions, I was able to work out a fee arrangement with the Congo family. The state of Virginia filed the necessary paperwork for his extradition, which we decided not to fight. Angelo was transferred to Norfolk, Virginia, to face charges of first-degree murder and armed robbery, both of which carry life sentences and the possibility of death by lethal injection. Since Angelo was from and the crime committed in Virginia, it was necessary to obtain the services of an attorney licensed in that state. We hired Nick William for the second chair. We filed all the necessary motions needed in this type of case. Interestingly, my first capital murder case occurred in my first year of practice.

Initially, Angelo claimed he was not the triggerman during our many discussions. I asked what happened on the day in question. Eventually, he told me the entire truth. He and the other defendants needed drug fixes and had no idea how to pay for them. So they decided to go to a neighborhood bank and watch customers withdraw monies from their accounts.

Angelo noticed a Filipino withdrawing a large sum of money. Angelo ran to the van to tell the other occupants. They followed him to his residence. Angelo approached the man, inquiring about a fictitious address. The man tried to give him directions but was unable to do so. Angelo pretended to leave. As the man placed his key into the lock, he turned to see Angelo walking quickly toward him. Angelo tried to overpower him, which resulted in a fight. Angelo pulled his gun and shot the victim several times during the struggle, killing him for the money. Angelo ran to the waiting van and divided the money equally with the others. The money did not last long because they used the money to purchase illegal drugs.

Someone recognized the license plate number of the van and reported it to local authorities. The authorities were on the lookout for the van. The driver of the van was arrested, and he implicated the other defendants involved. Angelo knew it was time to leave Norfolk. He first traveled to Miami, Florida, and then to Jackson, Mississippi. Later, he arrived in Baton Rouge and remained there until his arrest for a domestic dispute.

While Angelo was on the lam, his codefendants were making deals with the district attorney's office to turn state's evidence against him. In so doing, it was claimed that he was the triggerman. As such, he was indicted for first-degree murder and armed robbery.

After the motion hearings, we received Brady and Jencks materials. Under the Brady doctrine, the prosecutor is responsible for disclosing exculpatory information about the case, such as police reports, that may prove the defendant's innocence or the identification of another as the criminal perpetrator, that is, evidence favorable to the defense. Most of the defendants had already served their time except one, whose release date was within the year.

I made several trips to Norfolk to defend Angelo and discuss the logistics of his case with him and the cocounsel. As the lead attorney, it was necessary to inquire as to whether any deal was forthcoming, but the district attorney was adamant about prosecuting him. The community wanted justice. I sensed that the assistant district attorney might have contacted the Louisiana Bar Association to inquire about my standing with the bar and the number of years I had been a member. He felt he did not have to offer any deal because of my inexperience in handling a first-degree murder case.

Because of the inexperience, I worked ardently to prepare for trial. I must admit it created a financial hardship, causing me to shut down my practice to handle the demand of defending this case, not to mention the mental and physical drain. Yet I was determined to show the district attorney that I was a capable adversary despite the woes. I had to prepare for the case relying on promises for underwriting my expenses. I continued to read and study everything possible about first-degree murder trials. Although Congo's family had not tendered the financial obligations promised, I tried unsuccessfully to postpone the trial date until I could generate some needed capital. I went to William Ritize for assistance, and he lectured on how not to be conned by defendants and family members' promises. It was not a long lecture because he could see in my eyes how committed I was and how much I wanted to try this case. William made a signature loan for me at City National Bank to finance the trial.

With that, a thousand pounds of financial pressure seemed lifted off my shoulders, and I was able to prepare for trial. I spoke with attorneys who were learned in first-degree murder trials, such as those at the Southern Poverty Program and the Louisiana program for handling first-degree murder cases. I consulted with Michael Smalls, Robert Williams, Tony Marabella, and Robert Eames, all of whom have handled many first-degree murder cases.

For more than two months, I put my entire practice on hold while I defended this client. I honestly did not realize how much time and effort went into defending a client for first-degree murder. And financial issues continued. The week before the trial, the family sent travel fare, but they were unable to finance my stay in Norfolk while trying the case.

I flew to Norfolk, Virginia, for the trial. I asked if there had been any change of heart on the part of the district attorney's office, but he was still vehemently opposed to the offer. We had a few preliminary matters to resolve before the actual trial, which took about one day to conclude. The next day, the judge issued some dos and don'ts before voir dire.

In the first week, we selected only one juror. In the second week, we selected another prospective juror. The third week, the judge complained about how long jury selection was taking: "At the rate we are proceeding, it will take another month before the entire jury is seated."

I immediately cautioned the judge, "This is a first-degree murder case in which a man's life is at stake. Out of an abundance of caution, we, as members of the bar, have to do everything humanly possible to protect the defendant's constitutional rights."

The judge agreed by allowing us to proceed in the same fashion. Another juror for the panel was selected. From nowhere, just out of the blue sky, the assistant district attorney bent over and motioned to me. As I bent over to hear what he had to say, he whispered in my ear, "Would your client accept a double life with the opposition?" I was shocked and certainly caught off guard by his remark. I responded with a resounding no. Without thinking, I further told him that my client was not interested in any plea. No one had to tell me how stupid I was in not allowing my client to decide for himself. I know I had a legal obligation to do so, but I wanted my day in court. I was truly ready to try this case, and nothing was going to prevent me from doing so.

Another week passed, and we still had not selected another juror. Then assistant district attorney asked, "Would your client accept a double life without any opposition during his parole hearing?"

I reluctantly replied, "I will pass this information on to my client."

I knew I had to do what I was trained to do. I was obligated by law to present my client's cause and not to try to further my personal goals. I was there to represent him and only him to the best of my legal training.

At first, my client did not want to accept the offer. But I attempted to force him to accept the plea bargain. I emphatically told him, "You killed another human being who had a two-year-old child. The deceased will never be able to hold his child's hand or hug her in his arms when she is crying for her daddy. You, Angelo, on the other hand, will be able to see your son and probably be instrumental in his life upon your release from prison." As I explained to him, the other consideration was that "You are a first-time offender who makes you eligible for parole in seven years."

> The ethical considerations: Should an attorney attempt to postpone a trial because he or she has not received his attorney's fees?
>
> Should an attorney attempt to force a client to plead when the evidence is in favor of the state?

Should an attorney present an affirmative defense for the client when he or she knows the client was the triggerman?

Should an attorney withhold from the client an offer from the district attorney's office because he or she is interested in trying the case for his or her benefit?

Finally, should an attorney who has not acquired a year of practice try a first-degree murder case?

CHAPTER 4

The Ten Years and Six Months Rule

If a prisoner serves at least ten years and six months, and for the most part has been a model prisoner, he or she is eligible for early release despite the terminology of the statute of life without the benefit of parole, probation, or suspension of sentence. If a prisoner wants to avail himself or herself of the rule, a 10-6 motion must be filed in the court in which he or she was convicted. This motion will be decided on by the trial judge, the state attorney general, and the presiding judge during the trial. The three determine the fate of the convicted criminal.

State of Louisiana
Versus
Donald Robert Melancon

Shortly after finishing the Angelo case, my wife asked me to look in to her first cousin's case. I was a bit reluctant to do so, but I did anyway. I traveled to Ferriday, Louisiana, to retrieve the entire record before visiting Donald at the Louisiana State Penitentiary. The record was voluminous. It took weeks to digest the entire file, and there were many questions the file could not answer. The only person to answer these pressing questions was sitting in a cell in Angola, Louisiana.

I traveled to the prison to visit him and find answers to these perplexing questions before attempting to represent him in this matter. As I approached the entrance gates to the Louisiana State Penitentiary, a weird, unexplained feeling chilled my body. The guard checked my credentials and automobile. After a series of other delays, I was able to see Donald. My first impression of him was definitely correct. He was a smooth talker with one thing in mind—getting out of prison at any cost.

Donald had little or no remorse for his crime. He felt the world owed him an apology and that everyone, including his father, conspired against him by forcing him to plead to aggravated kidnapping and armed robbery. He could not understand how the codefendants were no longer in prison, but he was still incarcerated for his involvement. They had been released at least eight years prior to our first encounter. He was in the fourteenth year of his sentence.

I spoke with my wife and Donald's family about our conference. I felt extremely uneasy about representing him because of his attitude and the conflict it might present both ethically and personally. That is, should an attorney represent a close relative of his or her family? If so, what conflict of interest is present in representing a relative? What impact would it have on my family if the prosecution of the case proved to be futile?

With this in mind, I decided to speak with Donald once more before deciding whether to represent him in the matter. As I drove to Angola, a very vivid thought raced through my mind: *If an inmate tries to escape from Angola, he will have an awful task in doing so.* The person who was responsible for placing the prison in its present location knew exactly what he was doing. Angola abuts the mighty Mississippi River, which embraces both swamps and hilly terrain. The road to Angola has the same entrance and exit. It is a very narrow and winding road with three hundred-feet slopes at various intervals. A motorist can only drive at a top speed of ten miles per hour. The 18,000-acre site is probably one of the most beautiful stretches of property to behold, but the beauty of Angola seems to disappear with the presence of inmates working on this neatly manicured landscape with a garden hoe in one hand and shovel in the other. Angola is a maximum-security prison harboring some of Louisiana's most dangerous criminals. What is this facility's actual purpose, to harbor dangerous prisoners or to perpetuate another form of slavery? When you consider the fact that African Americans constitute more than 70 percent of all prisoners, it makes one wonder since American whites are involved in more crimes than any other race. The pivotal question is, why are there a disproportionate number of African American prisoners to white prisoners in the system? The sentence structure is manifested in the

Louisiana Code of Criminal Procedure by virtue of the hard labor provision at Angola.

These thoughts while driving sort of helped to break the ice when Donald and I met for the second time at Angola. The meeting went quite well, but I could not help thinking that the family may have spoken with him about my apprehension of representing him, especially due to his lack of remorse, my possible conflict of interest in representing him, and his arrogant attitude.

I sensed he was on his best behavior. I guess you can say I was sort of "conned" by Donald, but I was beginning to look forward to representing him in court. The prospect of another high-profile case would certainly boost my ego, not to mention my career. So you can decide who was conning whom? I certainly used this case as a stepping-stone. Therefore, I zealously prepared for Donald's hearing.

In 1970, Donald and three other defendants conspired to kidnap the young daughter of a prominent local attorney. He and another defendant were caught as they tried to flee pursuing police cars. The other occupant of the automobile returned fire on the police officers until he ran out of ammunition. They surrendered to the police officers, still in control and having custody of the two-year-old white girl. Probably because Donald was a lifelong resident of Ferriday, whose father and mother were respected members of the community, in the melee, he was the only one knocked unconscious by a deputy sheriff using the butt of his shotgun. When Donald awoke in the hospital, the coconspirator was dead.

Shortly thereafter, he reluctantly pleaded to the charges of aggravated kidnapping and armed robbery, both of which carry life sentences. Donald felt he was pressured into pleading because the judge and the district attorney promised him that if he pleaded, they would recommend his pardon after he served ten years and six months in prison.

The judge retired and the then district attorney became the judge, and no promised release was in sight after Donald served more than fourteen years in prison. He had filed several motions requesting release on the 10-6 concept but to no avail. After carefully studying the composition of the pardon board during that era and the present pardon board, I was ready to file the appropriate motion. A post-conviction motion was the most accessible road to travel as opposed to filing an appeal. The district attorney, John Schivellin, recused himself because he was the attorney who represented Donald for the aforementioned crimes. He respectfully requested that the state attorney general's office represent them in the matter. All the judges for the Parish of Concordia recused themselves. Judge Faulkien was the district attorney who prosecuted the initial case. The other, Judge Robert Gremillon, was a member of the defendant's father's church; Donald's father supported Gremillon in his candidacy for judge. The Louisiana Supreme Court appointed the Honorable Judge Lloyd Love. A hearing date was scheduled after many grueling hours of reading through old records, interviewing witnesses, and preparing for trial.

The trial lasted for one week, with retiring Judge James Bulton and Judge Faulkien testifying. They promised that if Donald was a model prisoner while incarcerated at Angola, they would recommend his pardon. Also, the then district attorney and a member of his immediate family testified as to the statements of the judge and the district attorney. Moreover, Donald took the stand in his own behalf and was very convincing as a witness. At this juncture, it should be pointed out that the pardon board was composed of the lieutenant governor, district attorney, and the presiding judge, unlike the present professional pardon board. Generally, if the judge or district attorney recommended that the defendant be pardoned, he or she is pardoned. The trial ended with the judge stating that he was taking the entire proceedings under advisement. In the meantime, a capacity audience nervously waited for the decision.

It was not until two months later that the judge rendered a favorable decision, stating that Donald pleaded to simple kidnapping. The armed robbery charge was dropped by the state. When Donald pleaded to the charge, he was immediately released from the parish prison in Concordia (where he was incarcerated until the judge ruled). He also had liberal visitation privileges while incarcerated in that prison. The surrounding community was aware of it.

Interestingly, the father of the kidnapped victim asked, "So you are Orscini Beard?" I replied in the affirmative. He gave me a respectable once over, which made me feel that I had done an admiral job in defending Donald in spite of his disdain for him. My nephew, Joseph Melancon, also gave me the impression that my representation of my wife's cousin was super. The judge and the entire district attorney's staff, along with the assistant state attorney René Solomon, complimented my performance. I responded by indicating, how much I learned from all of them in their presentation of the case.

> Should a district judge or a district attorney participate in the actual plea bargaining process by promising to assist the defendant before the pardon board if the defendant pleads to the charges prior to actually pleading? If so, to what degree can they participate in the plea bargaining process?

> Should the action of the district judge or district attorney be deemed inappropriate and, as such, construed as a form of coercion or duress? Should attorneys, judges, and district attorneys avoid the slightest form of impropriety?

> Should a defense attorney report the actions of the district judge and district attorney to

the Louisiana Bar Association? Is there a conflict of interest in representing a relative? Should an attorney further his or her personal interest or career by representing a defendant because it is a high-profile case?

Should a jury inform a defendant of his constitutional right of a trial, especially since the crimes charged are punishable by life imprisonment and, as such, the exposure is life if convicted and life if he or she pleads?

CHAPTER 5

The Jury Trials

State of Louisiana
Versus
Terri Priest

Terri, a twenty-one-year-old white woman with three young children, was indicted for second-degree murder in the death of her half brother. She allegedly gave an incriminating statement to a detective, who was later convicted of second-degree murder himself and is serving a life sentence as a result. The detective testified as follows:

> Terri and her brother were drinking and drugging all day and all night. He made several advances, but she joked them off.
>
> While sleeping, he caressed her private parts without any resistance whatsoever until she realized it was him. By that time, he had entered her vagina. She did not resist during the intercourse, because they had several focused sexual encounters in the past during her adolescence, resulting in violent physical abuse. Later, Terri fell into

a deep sleep, armed with a revolver. Several hours later, he wanted more sex from her, but this time an argument erupted to such a degree that she pulled a pistol, warning him to stop. He continued to make advance; Terri was unable to fight off his advance. He was shot several times in the chest area. He was hospitalized for several months until he succumbed to the gunshot wounds.

Before the trial, Terri discussed reasonable defenses. We reviewed her alleged incriminating statement in its entirety in conjunction with her taking the stand in her defense. After carefully addressing the issue, three pertinent facts emerged: (1) How to neutralize her use of alcohol and drugs before the jury without deliberately committing a fraud? (2) How to present Terri as being a physically abused youth whose family was dysfunctional without misrepresenting the truth? (3) How to twist and bend the truth to benefit Terri's defense without manipulating the justice system?

These questions were an affliction of the trial tactics. I knew Terri was going to be a dynamic witness. She was such a doll, whose misfortune was having grown up in a dysfunctional family where incest was a regular and frequent occurrence within the family. I was baffled. Should I try the case from a moralistic standpoint or a legalistic point of view?

If I did what the *Code of Professional Responsibility* dictates, this young woman would surely be convicted. If convicted, she could spend the rest of her natural life in prison for a crime that cried out for compassion. If any person ever merited a second chance, Terri fits the mold. A sentence for second-degree murder is mandatory; that is, the presiding judge has no discretion in sentencing. As such, he or she would have to sentence her to life imprisonment without the benefit of probation, parole, or suspension of sentence. This was not a case to win at any cost; it was a case to see justice prevail for a young woman who has been a victim of circumstances. It was a clear example of the lawyer's dilemma.

Hell, I was hired to deploy a defense of necessity! Indeed, the truth was stretched beyond the legal boundary, but by the same token, she was allowed to present an intelligent, plausible counterclaim to the charge. The saying that "There is no truth," does not imply that there are lies. With this in mind, I am cognizant of the story an old trial lawyer told: "If you are in a struggle with the district attorney's office and you bring a knife to a gunfight, you do not have to contemplate too long about the outcome of the fight."

The *Code of Professional Responsibility* requires an attorney not to present a deceptive defense. To do so would be a direct violation of the code above. Query: How does one justify the prospect of allowing Terri to go to prison for the rest of her natural life in light of this code?

Does the justification outweigh the responsibility of zealously defending one's client? The system sentences innocent defendants for telling the truth. Can attorneys prevent this inequity from happening? How would you represent your client under these circumstances? Given that there have been myriad questionable trial tactics used by the district attorney's office in representing the state in the past, disciplinary actions were null and void for their uses of the truth.

The case was submitted to the jury after a week of testimony. The jury deliberated for approximately ten to twelve hours before rendering a responsive verdict of manslaughter. The basis for the verdict was, as one juror said, "Even if we never really knew what did happen on that particular day, there were many instances in which we can be sure of what did occur to her sexually by her brother and therein lies the heat of passion doctrine. We felt this negated the specific intent to kill, required to render a second-degree murder verdict." Judge Robert "Bob" Hester was so impressed by our defense that he ordered a sentencing hearing. The sentencing hearing was tried for two days in which he took the testimony of the witnesses under advisement. In two weeks, he sentenced Terri to two years imprisonment. She had already been incarcerated for seven months. Thus, Terri was released within two months. Terri is now a legal secretary for a local law firm and has not been involved in any illegal activities since her release. She has been a model citizen and a pillar of the community. Terri is married and has reared her children of a prior marriage successfully. One of her offspring is a sergeant in the US Army.

Should the law be used as a pawn in a game?

Should an attorney use his or her moral or legal judgment in representing a client?

Should an attorney justify his or her representation by using the concept, "They did it, so can I"?

Is an attorney correct in his or her assessment of trial tactics to win at any cost, "in the search for victory as opposed to truth"?

If an attorney undertakes a defense that conflicts with the *Code of Professional Responsibility*, should he or she cease and desist regardless of the facts?

State of Louisiana
Versus
Eric Brown

The significance of this case involved a revenge murder. Eric's brother Frederick was killed in a struggle with another African American male. Frederick was stabbed several times after he had gotten the best of the killer. Eric's brother ran about two feet and fell dead in his arms. The murderer, Nathaniel (Nat), was indicted for second-degree murder, but after extensive negotiations, he pleaded to manslaughter and was given a four-month sentence. He was also given credit for time already served. He was immediately released from the East Baton Rouge Parish Prison.

Of course, this angered his family. Nat frequently hung out on the corners in Scotlandville, drinking wine and beer with other members of the neighborhood, bragging about how he killed Frederick. Eric and his other brother, John, decided to kill him. The plan was for Eric and John to wear all black, walk up to him while he was drinking, and shoot him. Eric and John repeatedly discussed this plan.

John was beginning to have second thoughts about killing Nat and wanted to back out of the plan. But Eric was extremely serious about killing Nat. On a very dark night, dressed in all black, he quietly approached Nat while he was drinking and talking about his encounter with Frederick. Eric shot and killed Nat within seconds. Rumors had surfaced about Eric's involvement. He and members of his family were questioned by law enforcement agencies about Nat's killing. Interestingly, it should be noted that no witnesses came forward to implicate Eric as the triggerman in the slaying.

John was also questioned about the killing and implicated Eric. Both were arrested for the murder. John was arrested for accessory after the fact, and Eric was arrested for second-degree murder. Subsequently, both were indicted for the crimes as mentioned previously.

I was hired by Eric's family to defend him. After speaking with Eric about the crime, I found that many questions needed to be answered before tackling this formidable burden. First and foremost was whether John would turn state's evidence against him? If so, how could his testimony be neutralized? Second, did I want to know the exact details of the murder? And finally, what ethical considerations are prevalent in a crime such as this as an officer of the court?

The *Code of Professional Responsibility* kicked in immediately. For example, is it acceptable to be overzealous in defending a potential client for murder? It is accepted by the *Code of Professional Responsibility*. Nevertheless, to what degree should an attorney be overzealous in defending a client? Regarding this question, I did not have a clue as far as the answer was concerned because of my limited experience in handling a murder case of this magnitude.

Inevitably, did I needed to resolve this complicated issue? Query: Should I do some research by using an old textbook and notes on the subject?

A theoretical approach may not always be the best way of handling a case like this, especially since realities often conflict with each other, causing an unfortunate mixture of the two. What should be done in this matter? I pondered over the matter until it hit me: Let me solicit the assistance of someone who has experienced this dilemma.

After disclosing the strategy to Robert Eames, I listened very intently to what he had to say, even though it conflicted with the strategy I had planned to use in defending Eric Brown. He reminded me that I was an officer of the court, and as such, I should not perpetrate a fraud upon the court. Further, he explained how information was provided by attorney-client privilege, and accordingly, such information cannot be divulged. "In some instances, it is much better to not inquire as to the facts and circumstances surrounding the crime in question because it does tie your hands in defending one the client," he said. "Certainly, the truth is a double-edged sword for defense attorneys."

What am I to do in trying to defend Eric Brown zealously? The dichotomy is the theoretical approach versus the reality of defending the client zealously. The two are a mixture of oil and water. However, the prospect of presenting a defense that is less than candor could result in suspension, disbarment, and/or incarceration for me.

Shortly after that, I was informed by the district attorney's office that John had pleaded to accessory after knowing that he will receive probation if he testifies truthfully against his brother. Moreover, I received Brady and Jencks materials from Assistant District Attorney Jessie Bankston in which another eyewitness implicated Eric as the shooter.

Interestingly, the other eyewitness, who was incarcerated, initially told investigating officers that he had not seen anything. He said, "It was very dark, and the shooter wore very dark clothing," and as such, he could not recognize him." It was not until this information surfaced that it was necessary to discuss the possibility of a plea. I offered to plead Eric to manslaughter, which was rejected by Bankston.

Then I informed him how the same district attorney's office allowed Nat to enter a plea of manslaughter for stabbing Eric's younger brother, which was certainly intentional and met all the requirements for a second-degree murder verdict. It was not justice, but am I to sit in judgment? The role of a defense attorney is to protect the defendant's constitutional rights.

Now I had to deal with the testimony of Eric's brother and the other eyewitness. A very foolish unethical thought came to mind. I inadvertently suggested to Eric that if his brother decided to disappear—or not appear on the day of the trial—his exposure at best, criminally speaking, would be a citation for contempt of court, which carries a sentence of six months or fewer. He could be sentenced to a term of at most five years if convicted of accessory after the fact, whereas the conviction of second-degree murder carries a sentence of life imprisonment without the benefit of parole, probation, or suspension of the sentence. Cannily, the only way Eric could be released from prison was through a pardon board hearing.

In the state of Louisiana, a life sentence means just that, life. Yes, I allowed my feelings to cloud my legal judgment. John did not appear on the day of the trial. The only testimony of significance was that of the other eyewitness, who testified as to why he did not come forward and the underlying reason for his testimony at the trial. He promised the mother of the deceased he would do so. Eric was convicted of second-degree murder.

John was later arrested for contempt of court and immediately he informed Judge L. J. Hymel that he was told that if he did not appear, it would assist his brother in his endeavor. John was given a suspended sentence in both instances. Consequently, I was ordered to testify before Judge Hymel as to my involvement with John's nonappearance on the trial date. I informed the court that I spoke to Eric about it but had no idea that John would not appear at trial. It was an inconsequential statement. I was not charged with a crime but realized how close I came to losing my freedom and license. Is there a thin line between practicing before the bar or being behind the bars?

State of Louisiana
Versus
Rosico Brown

After successfully defending a few criminal cases, I began to receive calls from potential clients all over the state. A case in point is Rosico Brown of Ferriday, Louisiana, charged with distribution of marijuana. He called the office for an appointment to discuss the likelihood that I would represent him. Indeed, the prospect of defending my first drug case was so overwhelming that I did not listen to the facts as intently as I should have during the conference. Had I done so, I would not have taken the case after receiving the Brady and Jencks materials from the district attorney's office.

They had an open-file policy. The information obtained through the discovery process indicated that the Sheriff's Department of Concordia correctly executed the search warrant. The witnesses were both skilled and experienced undercover agents from other parishes who made several purchases from Rosico and other occupants of the dwelling. In addition to this, Rosco and the other defendants made incriminating statements as to who owned the marijuana. That could present obstacles for the defense. The notion of being silent until you have contacted your attorney was absent in this case.

The whole state of affairs was a mess. Under no circumstances was this a case I could win from a defense standpoint. My reputation was, of course, my utmost concern because I was starting to be noticed by my peers and high-profile criminals. If I lost this case, how would it damage my career? To cut my losses, I offered to lead him to a responsive charge, which the assistant district attorney, Ronnie Macmillan, rejected harshly.

All other avenues were closed as far as receiving some relief from the motions filed. The inevitable was about to occur—another trial whose outcome was very bleak. I again tried to discuss a plea with both the district attorney and Judge Glenn Gremillion. The defendant immediately rejected the plea for the fifth time. I asked the judge, "If I tried this case, is his exposure a greater sentence for exercising his constitutional right to have a trial by a jury of his peers?"

"Of course not," the judge said. "This court does not penalize for exercising their constitutional rights." Seemingly, they were determined to take this case to trial to send a message to other dealers selling drugs in their community.

The trial of Rosico Brown began with many onlookers. I was neither ready nor prepared to defend him until we thoroughly went through each piece of evidence necessary to inject reasonable doubt in the jurors' minds. The reasonable doubt concept is another way of presenting the jury's stretched truth with emphasis on why this is not possible given the facts of the case. Is there an ethical consideration that a trial attorney should view before using this defense? Again, I had to present a defense of necessity. Am I paid to protect his constitutional rights? It was up to the state to prove its case beyond a reasonable doubt. If the state does not prove the case to the jurors' satisfaction, the defendant should be released. The state undoubtedly is endowed with enough financial resources and human resources to bring this case to a favorable conclusion. If the state does not do its job, I cannot do it for them.

We rehearsed the testimony of all the defense witnesses to such a degree that I started to believe there were reasonable doubts in this case. Although I was taking a risk by not allowing Rosico to testify, it was, nevertheless, a risk I was willing to chance. Because of a prior criminal conviction and demeanor, he would have enraged or isolated the white jurors. I was determined to present an intelligent, affirmative, and competent defense, void of lies.

The jury selection was a slow and tedious process. A week of picking and choosing prospective jurors ended with all parties relieved at the end of the formidable task. If ever a case favored the prosecution, the case of the State of Louisiana versus Rosico Brown certainly fits the mold.

It was an uphill battle with the defense doing everything humanly possible to discredit the state's key witnesses. And I did precisely that. I pointed out many inconsistencies by the key witness, who happened to be a blue-eyed white person. Mainly, I asked him, "Why would a person who had never seen you before and did not know you from the man in the moon sell you a couple of marijuana bags? He has always had a strong dislike for whites, which has been well documented throughout this trial by other key witnesses for the state."

His nervous response was, "I won his confidence."

I also asked the other crucial witnesses to locate Rosico's house on a map and what direction they proceeded to approach his house. I followed this by asking them to answer, "How were you able to gain entrance to Rosico's home without being noticed, especially since it was necessary to pass individuals stationed at the point of entrance and the corner for the expressed purpose of notifying Rosisco when there was a raid by the local authorities?" In other words, there was only one way in and one way out. Rosico's house abutted a levee. He had lived only in this house while growing up in Ferriday, Louisiana. He was extremely familiar with the levee, having played and traveled on it for years. "What prevented him from destroying the evidence before your arrival, when you gave notice of sirens' sounds?" These questions and the testimony of the defense witnesses and summation were sufficient to muddy the water for a responsive verdict of possession of marijuana, which in Louisiana is a misdemeanor.

Another victory for the defense. Interestingly, an African American alternate juror told me before leaving the courtroom that whatever verdict comes out from this trial, I had nothing to be ashamed of because I had done everything a person could do in defending his client. He and the other four black jurors were discussing how very proud they were of me in defending my client. I responded by saying, "If it was not for persons like yourself, struggling, I could not receive an opportunity for an education in order to try cases in this courtroom."

He replied, "You are right."

Yes, it was a very proud moment for me. Nevertheless, before this gentlemen's statement, Rosico had said that no matter what the verdict was, he wanted to shake my hand and hug me for doing what he knew no other African America attorney would have done. Despite all this, the highlight of the moment came when Judge Gremillion told the jury, "I have presided over several criminal cases, but never have I seen an individual who had nothing to hang his hat on defend his client with so much zeal, dedication, feelings, and competency. You are honor to your profession." The practice of criminal law is indeed a passion.

> Is it unprofessional conduct for a lawyer knowingly to use embellished information to create reasonable doubt?

> Is it unprofessional conduct for a lawyer knowingly to use false information to create reasonable doubt by employing, instructing, or encouraging others to do so?

> Is it unprofessional conduct for a lawyer to coach witnesses while on the stand by using leading questions?

Is it unprofessional conduct for a lawyer knowingly to cross-examine a witness by innuendo?

Is it the obligation of a defense lawyer to defend his client within the rules of the games?

Should an attorney conclude that a favorable verdict justifies all because that favorable verdict is the client's only concern?

CHAPTER 6

Drug Cases

State of Louisiana
Versus
Donald Lakeith Melancon

After the Rosico trial, my name was becoming a household word in the criminal community in general and in Ferriday, in particular. Donald was stopped while traveling north on I-61 with allegedly two ounces of powder cocaine. He had just left Natchez, Mississippi, heading toward Ferriday, when Deputy Sheriff Dave Cowen spotted his vehicle. Deputy Cowen immediately turned on the red and blue flashing lights along with his siren while his patrol car turned in pursuit of him. Donald nervously pushed the acceleration to the floor, trying to elude the officer and frantically emptying the substance from the plastic bags. Unfortunately, the wind engulfed the bag, blowing it right out of his hand. Unable to see where the bag landed, he decided to surrender to Officer Cowen after four other patrol cars joined the high-speed chase. Donald was handcuffed and placed in the patrol car's back seat after being carefully searched for a dangerous weapon. There was no cocaine discovered on Donald or inside his car, but Officer Cowen discovered traces of cocaine residue in a little white plastic bag located on the left bumper of his car.

At approximately 3:00 a.m., Uncle Thomas called me. He informed me that his grandson was arrested by Deputy Cowen of the Ferriday Sheriff Department for cocaine distribution. The next day, I canceled everything on my docket and rushed to Ferriday to investigate the legality of the arrest. As I drove to Ferriday, I thought of the first question a defense attorney asks—or should ask—in all drug cases: Was there a lawful purpose for stopping Donald on that particular night?

First, I spoke with Donald about the potential stop-and-frisk aspect that resulted in his subsequent arrest. He related the following information:

> He had just left Natchez, Mississippi, with two ounces of cocaine. As he entered the state line of Louisiana and approached Ferriday, he noticed Officer David Cowen. Officer Cowen also noticed him. They were heading in opposite directions when Officer Cowen immediately turned his patrol car around to pursue him. Donald said, "Of course, I decided to get rid of any evidence before surrendering. So, I poured out the cocaine while eluding him. I knew he didn't have any reason to stop me because

> I had not spoken to anyone about going to Natchez to score, or when I was going to leave to come back to Ferriday. Deputy Cowen stopped me simply because of my drug history with him.

After obtaining this information, I decided to visit the district attorney's office to discuss the case. There has always been an open-file policy adopted by District Attorney Johnny Jones. His assistant, Ronnie McMillian, has followed this policy to the letter. Assistant District Attorney McMillian opened his entire file, and I inspected the affidavit of probable cause for any flaws. If found, I would file a motion to suppress an illegal stop by Officer Cowen. The affidavit is merely a sworn statement given by the affiant or an informant stating that he or she has firsthand knowledge of a person in possession of an illegal drug substance.

As I read the affidavit, I found myriad questionable methods employed by the Sheriff's Department of Concordia Parish. Of significant importance was the use of an informant, which in this instance, allowed Officer Cowen to stop Donald on the night in question. Traditionally, an informant is anyone who has given information about a person to authorities that ultimately led to arrest and conviction of that person. Thus, any information given about a person's illegal activity in the future will become a reliable informant. As such, any law enforcement agency can go to a duty judge and request an affidavit of probable cause based on previous reliable information. The smaller parishes in Louisiana have liberally interpreted the term.

It is imperative to win a case during the preliminary stage of a criminal proceeding because a trial on the merits before a jury is a formidable task. A technicality or a loophole often used by television lawyers to increase the odds of a win is the filing of pretrial motions. During this stage, a lawyer is afforded an opportunity to find out what kind of cards the prosecutor holds; in other words, go on a fishing expedition. It is also used to determine if the informant's identity should be revealed because of specific constitutional issues. If so, is the evidence fruit of the poisonous tree? If so, it is likely inadmissible. Pretrial motions answer these questions and many more. Therefore, lawyers must understand the importance of proper research and skillfully drafted motions tailored to the investigation.

With this in mind, I filed motions tailored to what I determined to be an illegal stop by Officer Cowen and the setting of an unusually high bond. A separate hearing for a reduction in bond was held. I asked the duty judge ex parte to reduce the bond he initially set, but the district attorney's office got wind of what I was attempting to do. Assistant District Attorney Ronnie McMillian opposed the meeting.

As a result, I had to file a motion for a bond reduction. During the hearing, I reminded the judge and Ronnie that my client had never been convicted of any crime. Also, he had family in the community and deep-rooted ties to the parish.

Judge Glenn Gremillion set a more reasonable bond for Donald after a hard-fought oral hearing and well-pleaded motion with a supportive memorandum. The motion to suppress was scheduled for the next month. The hearing required two days. After my lengthy cross-examination of Officer Cowen, the judge ruled that the informant's identity had to be revealed for constitutional reasons. Primarily, the defendant is entitled to a fair and impartial trial. The involvement of the informant was so essential to the illegal transaction, the defendant could not receive a fair trial without his testimony. Under the Sixth and Fourteenth Amendments of the US Constitution, he would be denied a very fundamental right—the right to confront his accuser— by not allowing him the opportunity to cross-examine him as to the truth of the matter during the pretrial hearing or actual jury trial.

Before Officer Cowen revealed his source, Assistant District Attorney McMillan requested a short recess, which the judge granted. During the recess, I overheard Officer Cowen and Ronnie engaged in a profound discussion about their next strategic move regarding whether to reveal the informant's identity or drop the case. They were reluctant to reveal the informant's identity because doing so would seriously impede future and pending investigations of drug activities in the area. I walked outside the courtroom to find my client and tell him about the discussion. But before I could go into details, the judge called the court to order. I did briefly tell him of the district attorney's dilemma.

As Ronnie and I prepared to proceed with the motion to suppress, Ronnie requested a stay. It is merely a technique used to stop all proceedings until a higher court can determine if the request merits further consideration. If it merits consideration, then the court will decide the issue in question. The party requesting the writ is entitled to have the trial stopped by the Third Circuit Court of Appeals to decide if the lower court's ruling was correct in ordering Officer Cowen to reveal the identity of the informant because to do so may endanger him or thwart future or pending drug cases. Rushing to my feet, I almost lost my balance before I was able to object to the request. He already had an ample opportunity to assign error to the judge's ruling before requesting a recess. Failure to do so precluded him from now reserving the matter for the appeal. Furthermore, he was avoiding or stalling the inevitable. Of course, from a tactical standpoint, Ronnie was doing what he was being paid to do, protect the people of Louisiana. However, I could not help but wonder if he and the judge had some kind of discussion about not objecting to the ruling or requesting a stay to allow the Third Circuit to decide the question. These things often occurred in some of the outlying parishes. We argued various reasons back and forth, and in the process shouted at each other, until the judge told both of us to shut up and sit down. He announced he was taking the matter under advisement and angrily stormed off the bench. From a defense standpoint, it was a hollow victory. The end was in sight. My client was very emotional and happy about the outcome of the two days of hearings.

It was not until six months later that the judge ruled that Officer Cowen had to reveal the name of his informant. And within a few minutes, the assistant district attorney motioned to the court that he was dismissing the bill of information against my client. As such, Officer Cowen was no longer obligated to reveal the name of his informant. A bill of information is merely an accusation of a criminal charge for which someone is to be tried by the district attorney's office.

My client was elated with the final decision. It was not a victory because of the other possible defendants who might not be as fortunate as Donald LaKeith Melancon was on his days in court.

> Should an attorney reveal confidential information to his or her client that was overheard during a private conversation between the district attorney's office and another public official?

> Should an attorney investigate when he or she feels the district judge and assistant district attorney may have collaborated

about stalling a hearing to receive a favorable ruling on an issue, such as failing to object in a timely manner?

Should an attorney zealously request the informant's identity when doing so might cause harm to the informant and his or her family?

Should an attorney file a motion for discovery to find loopholes or technicalities in the proceedings in order to prevent his or her client from being tried by a jury?

Should an attorney accept money from a drug dealer when it is known it comes from ill-gotten gains?

State of Louisiana
Versus
Michael Anderson

I was on a roll; the dice kept coming up seven or eleven! Deputy Sheriff David Cowen had stopped Michael as he entered the Louisiana line from Natchez, Mississippi. Natchez is located next to Louisiana's state line in Vidalia. The same road is used to enter and exit both states. Perhaps there are other roads to use in traveling to Vidalia, but this route is the one most commonly used by drug traffickers.

Michael was arrested for the distribution of two pounds of marijuana. Again, the stop was predicated on information provided by a so-called reliable informant. A friend of the family contacted me about representing Michael. He was jailed under a $75,000 bond. Securing his client's freedom recognizes a defense attorney. Michael's case was allotted to the hardest and meanest of all the judges in the parish, Judge Fulkernihim. This was my first encounter with him, and everything that was said about him was indeed right. And from my viewpoint, more so. He had an aura about him. The only way an outsider could expect to receive any kind of favorable or preferential treatment was to be part of the good ole boy network. Since I was new to the area, I had to be extra careful not to offend him, primarily due to our previous confrontation during a postconviction hearing in the matter of the State of Louisiana v. Donald Robert Melancon. I must add, although congenial, it was an awkward moment for all parties concerned. I often wondered if Judge Fulkernihim harbored any ill feelings about having to testify in the matter.

He was a very arrogant witness and judge. How would I approach this man whose face and handshake were as stern as his decisions about my client's bond reduction? If he turned me down, what other legal recourse would I have since I had not filed a motion for a bond reduction? I was perplexed. And I knew my client was not going to be happy if I could not secure his immediate release, which I had promised to do.

Without thinking, I made an ex parte call to the judge, requesting that the bond be reduced to $10,000. The judge politely refused to discuss the matter unless the prosecutor was present. "Why haven't you filed a motion for a reduction in bond?" he asked. I knew right then and there that I had my hands full with this judge. There would be no concessions in this case, and his politeness was just an affront in terms of how he felt about an outsider coming to Vidalia to tell him how to run his court. *I better have my homework done,* I thought.

As I drove to Vidalia to file motions in the case, I thought about an old saying I have often heard: "There is more than one way to skin a cat!" How could I secure his freedom without filing and waiting for a motion date, which could take months? Then it came to me. I would ask Assistant District Attorney Ronnie McMillian about the possibility of reducing the bond to $10,000. In so doing, I suggested that a probation officer monitor him, and my client be charged a reasonable fee for the monitoring. Of course, the probation officer could randomly visit his home or request his appearance in his office. And he could be drug tested randomly.

Ronnie was delighted to support my unfiled motion. We took the proposal to Judge Falkurnihimemer, who seemed to be pleased with the restrictions placed on Michael's freedom and granted the reduction. Michael's father used the deed to his property to secure the $10,000 bond. He was released after spending several days in the parish prison. It was a sort of consolation for both the prosecutor and the judge; I took it in stride. I had to do something because my client was becoming frustrated and did not want to hear more excuses. So I knew if I filed a motion for a bond reduction, I would be placed on the back burner of the stove. And it would take months before a hearing date would be scheduled. Even if a hearing date was scheduled, given the demeanor of the court, the odds of being successful were slim to none. Although I had to compromise, it was done with the understanding of gaining more in the future from both the prosecutor and the judge.

Unlike the previous case, the stop in this case was done correctly. Deputy Cowen made sure that the same problem, which existed in Donald Lakeith Melancon's case, didn't exist in Michael's case. Any motions filed in this case would be perfunctory, at best, so I had to skin the cat another way. I knew a trial would result in a conviction based on the affidavit of probable cause.

The only other alternative would be a possible plea. After carefully discussing the same with my client, he agreed. We discussed offering a large fine to the state for a probated sentence. "How would you pay this fine?" I asked. He mentioned he had some money from his drug dealing hidden for a rainy day. Of course, I requested the remainder of my fee.

He reached behind the bar counter and pulled out a large black box filled with five-, ten-, and twenty-dollar bills. He counted out $3,000. I dared not ask the source of the money while sitting in his father's bar.

Likewise, Ronnie was interested in pleading the case. He did not want to take the chance of another trial. So he suggested a five-year prison sentence, suspending all but one year. I rejected the offer without telling my client.

I suggested that we table the offer for about six months to determine if my client had any more brushes with the law. We rescheduled the matter for a status hearing in eight months. I can't take credit for the unexpected result at the status hearing. I suggested to Ronnie that my client be fined heavily and placed on probation for two years, and if he did not violate any criminal laws in those two years, he would be granted an Article 893. An 893 is not automatically granted, but when given, a first-time felon can have his or her criminal conviction expunged or purged from the records of the clerk of court if the individual stays free from any criminal activity during the specified period. Thus, the judge sentenced him to two years with the Department of Corrections. He suspended the two years and placed him on supervised probation for two years. He was also fined him $3,000, which my client was happy to pay—and did pay in three equal installments, along with his supervision fee. I was again given praise for my performance in defending Michael Anderson.

Should an attorney engage in an ex parte conversation with a judge?

Should an attorney inform his client of any plea bargain offered by the prosecuting attorney?

Should an attorney suggest a large fine when he or she knows the client will use illegal drug money to pay the fine, which has not been taxed by the IRS to limit exposure to incarceration?

Should an attorney make promises in criminal cases?

Should a client be penalized for the actions of his or her attorney?

Should a judge refuse to reduce a bond based on the attorney's demeanor or consider the factors detailed in the *Louisiana Code of Criminal Procedure*?

Should an attorney decline payment of his or her legal fee because drug money is used?

State of Louiana
Versus
Larry Williams

Ellison O'dneal, a dear friend of mine who attended law school with me, called about a close friend of his who had been arrested for possession of marijuana. In Louisiana, possession of marijuana carries a penalty of six months in jail or a fine of $500 or both. I asked O'dneal why he hadn't obtained the assistance of counsel in his city of Alexandria, since it was a misdemeanor. O'dneal said, "He is charged as a second offender, which carries a stiffer penalty than a first offender." We continued to discuss the case, when O'dneal made a revelation about his drug activities and how the local authorities were determined to bust him at any cost.

Larry had as many as twenty pit bulls that were allowed to roam freely. When local officials wanted to raid his premises because of alleged drug activities, they had to secure the dogs before entering. Of course, this allowed him an opportunity to dispose of any drugs or drug paraphernalia in or surrounding his premises. It made them extremely displeased, and if they could charge him with any criminal violation, it was not beyond them.

On this occasion, local authorities decided to conduct a raid on his premises, but the pit bulls proposed a problem. The noise they made alerted Larry. He jumped to his feet and ran with an unspecified amount of crack cocaine to the bathroom, but his water was turned off, preventing him from flushing the substance down the toilet. He quickly ran to the back bedroom to dissolve the crack cocaine, when the local authorities yelled on the horn, "If you want your dogs, please come out and put them on a leash." Instantly, he dumped the crack in a preconstructed container for dissolving it. He retrieved a marijuana roach on the table from the previous night.

Larry came out of the house to put his dogs on leashes. The officer in charge informed they had a warrant to search for illegal drug activities. They searched the house and the grounds but were unable to find any crack cocaine. However, an officer did find the visible marijuana roach on the table. He was arrested and booked into the parish prison for possession of marijuana.

Larry was able to make bail without my assistance. He wanted to discuss the case with me as soon as possible, so I scheduled a meeting for the next week. We met for approximately two to three hours, discussing the ramifications of his arrest and why he was charged as a second offender. After the meeting, I filed several motions for discovery concerning his first conviction of possession of marijuana. The district attorney's office has an open-door policy, so they sent me their entire file on Larry.

After carefully reading the minutes of the first conviction, I concluded that the presiding judge did not inform him of the enhanced penalty provision if he pleads. Failure to inform him could result in that conviction being overturned. As such, he could only be tried as a first-time offender. The length of the sentence enhances the penalty. The punishment escalates from six months to five years of incarceration. Since they were determined to try him as a second offender, it was my duty to challenge the first conviction.

With this in mind, I filed a motion to suppress the first conviction because he was not informed of the enhanced penalty provision, as previously mentioned. The hearing was held for several hours, and the judge ruled in favor of the defense. When then offered to plead as a first offender, but the judge was determined to sentence him to six months. "Judge, I might as well try the case, since you have already indicated that you'll sentence him to six months, which is the most he can receive under the statute," I stated.

"Of course, that might be so. But if you try this case, he'll receive six months most definitely," the judge replied.

"But, Judge, how can you give a person six months without hearing the evidence?"

"Oh, I am going to hear the evidence. But after the trial, he's going to jail for six months."

"No presentence investigation?"

"No. Why waste the state's money? He's going away for six months, so the ball is in your court. But he can do his time on the weekends, and I will give him two months to get his affairs in order."

"What if I file an appeal after the hearing?"

"Go ahead, but it will take about six months to a year to hear the appeal. And by that time, he would have done the six months imposed by me."

"What about three months, Your Honor?"

He nodded.

In a sidebar, Larry and I discussed the judge's adamant stance. I told him I would not try the case knowing the preconceived notion of the judge. Larry wanted to file an appeal, so I had to explain to him how long it would take an appeal to run its course. I also told him how he could do his time in the parish prison. "Oh, the judge mentioned to me that you are an A-1 mechanic, and you could work on some of the patrol cars. And he will give you some additional time off for doing so." Larry accepted the plea.

The judge Boykinized Larry and thoroughly explained the enhanced penalty provision. Larry was sentenced to three months with credit for time served. And as promised, he was allowed to go home for three months to get his affairs in order.

Should a judge force a defendant in to a plea? If so, should the lawyer bring such an action to the attention of the judicial committee?

Should a lawyer urge his or her client's cause and not be intimidated by the judge's preconceived notion of sentencing the individual's maximum sentence under the statute?

Should a lawyer bring charges against the judge for his or her bias?

Should a lawyer try a case knowing fully that to do so would be a helpless cause, and the client's interest can be best served by using a commonsense approach given the climate or attitude of the community?

Should a lawyer have a sidebar with a judge without having the conversation transcribed by the court reporter?

Should a lawyer urge his or her motions to determine whether the search warrant was valid while knowing the disposition of the court?

CHAPTER 7

Malfeasance in Office

State of Louisiana
Versus
Cynthia Porche

I had been handling so many criminal cases they were beginning to tax me. The calls were mounting, my caseload was increasing, and it was time to stop accepting new clients. I was tired of the client who always said, "Man, they got me wrong. I didn't do it." When was this madness going to stop? Most of my clients were guilty as sin, but to hear them tell it, they were not.

Then Cynthia Porche walked into my office. "May I help you?" asked my secretary. She wanted to talk to me about handling her case. "Mr. Beard is not accepting any new cases," Erica said.

"I was told that he would accept my case," said Cynthia, "Rose Richard sent me."

"Mr. Beard, Mrs. Richard sent her," explained Erica.

"But I'm not accepting any new clients until I reduce my caseload."

Immediately, Cynthia started crying. She had heard so much about me, and she wanted no other attorney to represent her in this matter.

"Mr. Beard, will you please at least talk to her?" Erica asked. So I spoke with her.

I had read numerous newspaper stories about how this social worker was negligent in the performance of her duty. I watched television reporters talk about the death of Joshua Ganeige. As the story unfolded, this social worker was the target of criticism from national and state media. A month before his untimely death, Cynthia had been sent several pictures of a two-year-old white boy whose body was marked with scores of scars. The boyfriend had repeatedly beaten Joshua. This information was communicated to a hotline and documented on an "alter sheet." It was then passed on to the department responsible for handling such cases. The case was allocated to one of the two supervisors. The supervisor would then assign the case to a social worker. In Joshua's case, that was Cynthia.

Cynthia made several visits to Joshua's home. Each time, his appearance was acceptable. She noted on the file that there were no visible signs that he was abused. Shortly after that, Cynthia received a telephone call from a neighbor who refused to identify herself. She told her Joshua was being neglected and abused. So Cynthia made another visit to his home. There was nothing to indicate the child had been abused. She did, however, discuss the situation with Madeline Korn, her immediate supervisor, but to no avail.

A week later she received the previously mentioned pictures, which she took to the supervisor on duty as Madeline was out sick. The duty supervisor was having problems with the social workers under her supervision. When Cynthia asked what she should do about the pictures, the supervisor said she had some pressing problems to deal with, and they would discuss the matter later. Cynthia stored the pictures in her desk, waiting for further directions.

Cynthia worked in crisis intervention, which meant that every case was equally important. There were several cases on her caseload requiring immediate attention. However, weeks passed with the little child being subjected to the same abuse. Unfortunately, Cynthia had forgotten about the pictures or that the supervisor on duty was supposed to get back with her to discuss what action, if any, should be taken. Madeline had not returned to work due to her illness. Another incident involving Madeline had been swept under the rug before the Joshua incident surfaced.

Meanwhile, Cynthia was working as hard as ever to assist her other clients. She spent many hours after work and on weekends trying to keep up with her overwhelming caseload. Under state law, a social worker is allowed only eighteen cases before more can be allotted to him or her.

When the social worker completes a file, he or she is given a new file, and the process is repeated. At the time of Joshua's death, Cynthia was handling approximately fifty-two cases.

Cynthia was both respected and hated by her peers because of her dedication to her clients and in her persistence in asking questions of the supervisors during meetings. Because of her questions, meetings often ran over their scheduled times, long past when her colleagues were ready to leave. But she would not stop until her concerns were adequately answered. Her work did not go unnoticed by her immediate supervisor as substantiated by her evaluations.

Both the national and local press ambushed Cynthia. She was being painted as an unconcerned and heartless person. Indeed, Governor Edwin Edwards wanted her head on a platter. Shock waves were sent all over the country. There was a need to revamp the procedure in managing crisis-intervention cases, and Cynthia Porche was at the root of the problem. The community cried for her prosecution. A grand jury was impaneled. Within a week, Cynthia was indicted for malfeasance in office.

It was indeed a change of pace for me to represent an innocent person—finally. Yes, it was refreshing to represent a scared, loving, caring, and dedicated woman whose only desire was to be the best social worker in Baton Rouge. She had graduated with honors from Southern University's School of

Social Work. She was first in her family to graduate from college. Cynthia did this while rearing an eight-month-old boy.

This case was very technical, and I had a worthy adversary in Assistant District Attorney Michael Erwin. We had battled before in the matter of the State of Louisiana v. Terri Priest, so I was fully aware of his capabilities. My task was formidable, and I knew it. How would I defend her, considering the publicity disseminated by both the local newspaper and television stations?

Based on the publicity, Cynthia could not receive a fair trial in this city. But before I could file a motion for a change of venue, I needed to poll or survey the community to inquire about their knowledge of the Joshua Ganeige case. I had to subpoena the records of the local newspapers and television stations to determine the number of times a story about Cynthia was broadcast on radio or television news or mentioned in a newspaper column.

Once all the variables were intact, I filed my motion for a change of venue. Before the hearing, Mike asked me whether my client would accept a misdemeanor charge. I relayed the information to Cynthia, but she instantly declined.

When I arrived, the courtroom was crowded with newspaper and television reporters. The hearing lasted two days, with the judge taking the issue under advisement. Three months later, the judge ruled in favor of a change of venue based on evidence presented at the hearing. The trial was moved to Amite, Louisiana, and assigned to Judge Henry Causey. A status conference was held to set a trial date and clear up any ancillary issues. Mike again asked if Cynthia would accept a misdemeanor plea. I did not tell her about the offer because I really wanted to prove her innocence. She was a bundle of nerves and on the verge of having a breakdown if touched slightly. I often consoled her as she cried in my arms. I could not risk losing her at this stage of the proceedings. The stakes were extremely high because this case was more than just about Cynthia Porche. It was the system being on trial. A great deal of time and effort had been invested in my preparation of the case.

My family moved out of the house; I was a very unpleasant person while preparing for trial. I interviewed more than a hundred witnesses and read more than four thousand pages of information. I was beginning to catalog the report, which was immensely technical. Cynthia was as ready as she could be. It was showtime!

The trial took place in one of the smallest parishes in Louisiana. The courtroom was filled to capacity with spectators and the media. Perry Mason's cases could not match the audience in this trial. Judge Causey was retiring at the conclusion of this case, after thirty years of public service as a state representative and a judge.

It took two weeks to select a jury of six persons. The composition of the panel was all white except for one African American female. The trial was a dogfight. I used every trick in the book of trial tactics. I even went so far as to call then Governor Edwards and Governor Treen to establish the pecking order of how the system works regarding child protection. The department heads and divisional heads were also called as prospective witnesses.

Conversely, the testimony dealt primarily with how the department *should* operate as opposed to how the department *was* working. I was able to solicit statements regarding how crises-intervention workers were trained and for how long. Witness after witness testified that there was no formal training manual, but training was done on the job for about two weeks. After the training period, they were given a caseload of eighteen cases. Either the supervisor or a senior crisis worker resolved any problems. Many crisis workers were either burned out after a year or transferred to other departments. The social worker's caseload could soar to as many as fifty cases (or fifty-two in Cynthia's case) though the manual places a limit of eighteen cases per social worker.

It was proven that Joshua's case was listed as one to watch before Cynthia was assigned to the case. Other social workers higher on the totem pole than Cynthia had knowledge of Joshua's situation, but they did nothing for him. There were several deficiencies in the department. Witnesses testified that on several occasions, department and division heads were informed by field workers of these deficiencies, but they failed to implement corrective procedures. The department was a time bomb, clicking, clicking, and clicking. It just happened to explode in Cynthia's face.

The trial was in its sixth week, and the case turned on two factors: Cynthia testifying on her behalf and the closing arguments of the defense attorney. Cynthia testified that she had only been employed for three months when she was suspended because of Joshua's case. The jurors cried and wiped their eyes as Cynthia spoke to them. If she knew that a child needed her, she would have come running because she had a child the same age as Joshua.

In the defense's closing statement, he expressed his disdain for the system, stating, "I don't know what's right or wrong, but I do know one thing: She has no business whatsoever sitting at this table by herself as the only person responsible for the death of Joshua Ganeige and malfeasance in office. The entire community is responsible. The neighbor who refused to identify herself, the intake worker who received the first telephone call concerning him, and even the supervisor who knew of Joshua's situation but was too concerned about her staff. They are all responsible. The immediate supervisor who was burned out knew about it but was too greedy to retire from the position. The seasoned veterans who did nothing to encourage Cynthia or offer advice when confronted with such a situation. And last but not least, the state of Louisiana for allowing the department to continue to function at a low level when they knew—or should have known—the consequences of underfunding the department."

Cynthia was found not guilty in forty-five minutes of deliberation.

There were so many newspaper articles, television reports, and interviews about the trial, Cynthia, and me. Most of the stories were favorable, though a few seemed to be disappointed by the verdict for this overworked, burned-out, and underpaid former social worker.

I was concerned about my client's mental state. Even though the trial ended, the stigma of failing to do her job permeated. A civil service hearing denied her claim for reinstatement when other successful defendants in criminal cases were automatically reinstated on request.

> Should an attorney inform his or her client of any offer to a plea from the prosecuting attorney if the client declined the first offer?

> Should an attorney defend a cause or the client?

> Is the client's interest more critical than a reason?

State of Louisiana
Versus
Allen Miller

Ellison O'dneal, a law school classmate, asked if I was interested in expanding my practice to a rural area. He had several cases that needed a lawyer with some courage to handle these controversial cases for the community. The facts never amounted to much, but they were, nonetheless, an opportunity to spend time in the country and serve a community that has been deprived of representation.

At night, I was able to relax in the cold, fresh, night air without the necessity of an air conditioner. The sheets on the bed were dried in the summer's sunny breezes. The pillows were made of real feathers. You could genuinely relax after a hard day of work in the field while riding a horse. It was life.

I enjoyed the atmosphere so much, I made it a point to travel to Colfax, Louisiana, at least once a week to consult with prospective clients. I managed to appear in court on a few routine matters, but I was cautious not to handle any case that required too much of my time. I still had a heavy caseload waiting for me in Baton Rouge. However, this proved futile when Judge Billy Lute appointed me to defend an elderly gentleman charged with the aggravated rapes of his great-grandnieces. I was shocked by appointment. I felt that my nexus to the court was minor. Why me when there were so many other able attorneys in Colfax to handle a case of this magnitude?

I later learned that Judge Lute wanted to appoint a local attorney. But since two minor children were involved, and my practice was very limited in the Colfax area, I would not be in as much jeopardy as a local attorney. The attorney's fee was set at $500 for defending my appointed client. Perhaps this was the real reason others had not taken the case. It would cost me several thousand dollars to defend him, not to mention the loss of other potential cases.

I tried every trick in the book to get out of representing this old white man charged with such a heinous crime. I did not like rape cases, but the defendant was entitled to representation, just as any other defendant. But I certainly did not want to represent him. I filed a motion to withdraw, which was heard the next week. Judge Lute denied my motion and set the trial date for the next month. He gave me a week to file any other pretrial motions. The district attorney allowed me to inspect his entire file, so there was no need to submit any additional motions. But four weeks was not enough time to prepare for trial. The judge's order was apparent—be in court or jail.

I stayed with Ellison a week before the trial to prepare properly. I needed to have access to my client. There was lots of information and questions that needed to be clarified and answered. Night and day, we labored over the information provided by the district attorney's office. The pivotal question of the children's ability to testify because of their tender age also needed to be resolved. We were looking for a needle in a haystack. What possible defense could I present to the jury?

Jury selection took longer than I anticipated. We finished selecting the last alternative juror on the third day of voir dire. Opening statements were to begin immediately after a thirty-minute recess. I waved the opening statement until after the prosecutor presented his case. The jury was dismissed for the evening, while we took care of some routine matters. Particularly, whether the victims were too young to testify. The judge ruled that the issue would be resolved before their possible testimony.

The trial was moving quite fast. It started turning in our favor when the investigating officers failed to dust an object for fingerprints, and the medical record indicated that the victims contracted gonorrhea, while my client tested negative for gonorrhea. The question foremost on my mind was how to introduce the medical records of the victims into evidence. It is necessary to lay the proper foundation for such testimony; consequently, there is an exception to the general rule that requires the attorney to follow specific regulations per the *Louisiana Code of Criminal Procedure*. Much of the testimony was routine until the victims were called to testify. I immediately objected to the call of the witnesses to the stand without it being determined if they were competent to testify. The jury was retired to the jury room until this matter was resolved. The judge ruled they were qualified to testify, but he cautioned us to handle them with gloves.

It was then that I was able to introduce each victim's medical records and the disease they contracted from having sexual intercourse with whomever. Moreover, their testimony was very incoherent and unintelligent, so the prosecutor rested his case.

I called only one witness, my client. He testified about what happened on that particular day. He also testified as to the result of his gonorrhea test. In fact, he tested negative to any disease. The jury voted 9 to 3 in our favor to acquit the defendant. The case was never retried, and the defendant was set free the same day, after spending a year in jail. He was sixty-seven at the time. The state paid me $500 for my services, and he paid me $3,000 to do the best job I could do.

> Should an attorney decline to represent an indigent client because the fee is not sufficient to cover expenses?

> Should a nonlocal attorney be compelled to accept appointment to a client when local attorneys are available to do so?

> Should an attorney receive a case on a pro bono basis?

Should an attorney take fees from both the state and the client? If so, is there an obligation or a duty to disclose the acceptance of such a payment from each?

Should an attorney refuse to accept an appointment to a case when there is not a legitimate reason to do so?

Should an attorney argue frivolous reasons before the court for declining an appointment simply because he or she does not want to take the case?

Should an attorney represent a client zealously?

CHAPTER 8

Death Penalty Cases

State of Louisiana
Versus
Sharon Morris

A former client referred Sharon Morris, a white female, who was charged with first-degree murder. Sharon was only eighteen years old. She and two other persons were involved in the shooting death of a forty-eight-old owner and manager of a used-car lot. Sharon prostituting herself with him. From her past experiences with him, she knew he always kept a large sum of money in his home. The mark (someone who has sex with another person for money) often flashed a wad of large dollar bills. Then he would peel off several hundred dollars to show her how much money he had. Sharon had been in his home several times. To rob him after having sex with him would cause a problem. If she tried to rob him, he would know that she set him up for the robbery. It was necessary to kill him herself.

All three of them went to his home. Sharon entered, while the others remained outside in the van. After thirty minutes, Sharon fired several shots, and her mark was dead. The codefendants then entered the home of the victim and ransacked it for money and valuables. They left, leaving the victim bleeding from his wounds. The victim died due to blood loss.

One of the defendants was arrested in Mississippi with the stolen automobile and in possession of stolen items. A check of the items revealed they were taken from the victim's home in Baton Rouge. Baton Rouge detectives traveled to Mississippi to interview the arrestee about the murder of the used-car lot owner. After an intense interrogation, the defendant revealed that he and two other defendants were involved because they needed money for drugs, and Sharon Morris was the one who shot the man.

The investigator arrested Sharon's boyfriend before arresting her. The boyfriend gave a statement implicating her as the mastermind behind the robbery and killing; that is, she killed the victim. Shortly after that, she was arrested and charged with first-degree murder. Sharon asked me to represent her after talking with Terri Priest. We never discussed fees because I knew she was unable to pay. I also knew that Sharon was the shooter without her confirming the same. But I wanted to represent her. She was only eighteen with her whole life ahead of her. I felt if I did not represent her, no one else would do an adequate job.

I filed some motions, including one stating the death penalty constituted cruel and unusual punishment. Prem Burns, who was prosecuting the case, answered immediately, and a hearing was scheduled in a week. We argued the motions filed. We also included lengthy affidavits from experts and attorneys who had appeared before the US Supreme Court explaining the same. The court ruled in favor of the state, and a trial date was set. However, we had other motions to be handled before the trial date. The motion hearing took many months and days to finish.

Months passed before a new trial date was set. After repeated discussions, Prem decided to offer us a deal. If Sharon accepted responsibility for the murder, she would be willing to withdraw her motion to seek the death penalty. But Sharon continued to claim that her boyfriend was the triggerman. I decided to review the boxes of information provided by the district attorney's office. In a file, her boyfriend made a statement that solidified his position that he was there just for the money and drugs. His only desire was to rob the man of his money so he could purchase drugs, after which he planned to leave Sharon. She knew he didn't love her but did everything humanly possible to win back his love and affection. She was also willing to prostitute for him, but he declined because he was frightened of her. I confronted her with his accusations. Sharon did not have to respond because the expression on her face told the story. "You can't continue to allege your innocence when your life is at stake," I said.

This discussion went back and forth for approximately two months. Then I received a call from Sharon; she wanted to see me at once. I quickly went to the parish prison to see her. As I entered the correction facility, I noticed Sharon crying in the side of the room. A guard was consoling her. As I entered the room, she immediately ran to my waiting arms. "I want to plead," she said, sobbing. "It is time to get this thing behind me. I want to apologize to the victim's family for killing him. And I ask God for his forgiveness." I was so shocked and impressed. What made her change her mind?

Without delay, I called Prem and told her we had a deal. "Can we set the plea for tomorrow before she changes her mind again?" Prem scheduled her plea for the next day. Judge Michael McDonald accepted her plea after a lengthy Boykinization. He asked whether I discussed the ramification of a guilty plea. I told her to say yes to the judge's questions without a detailed explanation. Sharon was given a life sentence without parole, probation, or suspension of sentences. Her only recourse is a possible pardon from the governor of Louisiana.

> Should an attorney force a client into a plea when the evidence is not in his or her favor?

> Should an attorney accept a plea without discussing the matter with family members when the defendant is of a young age?

> Should an attorney explain the ramification of a guilty plea involving a first-degree

murder case when not to do so would impede the client's ability to enter such a plea, even though it is in his or her best interest to do so?

State of Louisiana
Versus
Henry Bennett: Trial One

My practice was moving at a swift pace, and I was at the brink of success. I was doing well, and my peers knew it. I was glowing in the sun and didn't want to take another significant case until I had an opportunity to rest from the previous cases. Then a very gentle and warm woman walked into my office and asked if I would represent her son. She was so kind, I could not refuse her request—until she started to explain her son's crime. Fourteen-year-old Henry was charged with the raping and killing of a six-year-old boy. It made me sick to my stomach, having a six-year-old son myself. But Bertha's charm and sincerity convinced me to take the case despite the comments of associates in the firm and newspaper articles concerning the death of the child.

Another thirteen-year-old youth claimed he and three other kids sexually assaulted and killed him. Initially, they took him behind a building located in Mall City, where, he was raped and thrown down a fifteen-foot ravine. He did not die as a result. So Henry climbed down into the fifteen-foot ravine and dragged him back up to the surface. According to the youth, they dragged him two hundred to three hundred feet to another location in Mall City. He was then beaten severely and thrown into a swimming pool behind an apartment building. He cried profusely while they threw a heavy chair on top of his head. A man from the apartment complex noticed them by the swimming pool and asked what they were doing? The youths quickly scattered, leaving the little child to drown.

After many hours of the child being absent from the home while the skies grew darker, the grandmother knew that something awful had happened to her grandson. She and other family members roamed the neighborhood, looking for him. Hours passed, but they could not find the child. A cry went out, and the entire community rallied together to search for the little fellow. They walked every street of Mall City in search of him, but to no avail. Desperate, they asked if anyone had seen the child.

The thirteen-year-old so-called witness participated in the search, pretending to look for the child. The child remained missing until that next Saturday morning, when a tenant noticed a child floating at the top of the pool. The boy was submerged for three days. The news dampened the hopes of the citizens of Mall City and Baton Rouge.

The little child's older brother told local authorities that he saw his little brother playing with the thirteen-year-old

. the corner grocery store. After the news, the teen ran away from home and hid in an abandoned building for days. A caretaker of an apartment complex notified the city police about a child matching the description of the runaway was living in the abandoned building. The police officer discovered the thirteen-year-old and asked what he was doing there. As the officer began to speak, he saw out the apartment's window Henry Bennett and three others stealing an automobile from the parking lot.

The youth was taken to police headquarters and questioned about running away. He was asked if he had any knowledge of the disappearance and killing of the child. He immediately requested the presence of his uncle and his mother. When they appeared, he began to tell juvenile officials about events leading to the child's death. In so doing, he implicated Henry and the other youths. He described how and why they killed the boy. Within minutes, Henry and the other kids were in custody. The thirteen-year-old knew Henry and the other youths because they had a class together. But he mainly knew Henry from a fight they had a week before the incident. Henry hit him in the jaw when he was not looking. Interestingly, the thirteen-year-old youth was at least six feet tall.

The juvenile court transferred Henry to adult court within months of his arrest. Shortly after that, an East Baton Rouge grand jury indicted him for first-degree murder, and the district attorney's office opted for the death penalty. I filed a multitude of motions, including a change of venue. Judge Freddie Pitcher denied most of my motions, though he allowed us the opportunity to put on evidence for change of venue. However, after a trial run of prospective jurors, a majority of them indicated they could be fair and impartial.

With this in mind, we began to try the case. There were hundreds of newspaper articles and television reports about the incident. These articles and reports supported our change of venue motion. The judge took the hearing under advisement but ruled against us. Judge Pitcher did rule in favor of the jury viewing the scene of the crime. At the scene, they were able to discern whether Henry Bennett was capable of doing all the acts of which he had been accused.

It took approximately three weeks to sit one juror. It was a tedious task, but it proved to be the difference in a verdict of guilty.

We were able to secure all the police reports from an unknown source, and they were vital to our defense. Under state law, we are only entitled to the initial investigative police report concerning the crime. By law, we were not allowed any subsequent investigative police reports. At one point, the assistant district attorney, Thomas Walls, noticed the investigative police reports and said he would be interested in obtaining those reports. The jury was able to visualize the actual events that led to the child's death, nd more important, whether Henry was able to throw the victim down the ravine and pull him back up.

In fact, due to the police reports, we were able to contradict the testimony of the critical witness about what happened and the extent of my client's involvement in the crime. In addition, they were used to establish the whereabouts of my client at the time of the killing and to show how the youths ran in the same direction after committing the hideous crime. Common sense tells you that when children are doing something wrong or illegal, they will not run in the same direction. More often than not, they run in different directions.

When the jury visited the scene of the crime, they were able to follow the trail the youths took the child. The jury was also able to view the nineteen-foot ravine into which the child was thrown but not injured. Again, the investigative police reports assisted our defense because we were able to point out certain discrepancies. Notably, the little child was not injured. Nor did he break a leg or an arm due to the long fall. The child was crying after being thrown into the ravine. Henry climbed down the drop and carried him back to the surface, thus carrying him off to his destination, which resulted in his death.

After six weeks of trying the case, the jury was hopelessly hung 9 to 3 in favor of the defense.

Should a lawyer use an illegal source that may prove a client's innocence?

Should a lawyer decline a case because it's unpopular?

State of Louisiana
Versus
Henry Bennett: Trial Two

Baton Rouge was in an uproar after the verdict, and the city was calling for a conviction by exerting internal pressure on the then-district attorney Bryon Bush. Comments about the decision were either printed or televised daily. The pressure was intense on the district attorney's office to try Henry a second time. District Attorney Bush opted for a second trial. The publicity of retrying the case was so widespread, I decided to refile my motion for a change of venue. The motion hearing lasted several days. This time, Judge Fred Pitcher ruled in favor of the defense, and the trial was moved to New Orleans.

The district attorney's office decided to try the defendant for second-degree murder instead of the first degree. The reason for this was due in part to the jury. In a first-degree murder case, all twelve jurors must vote unanimously. In a second-degree trial, the jury needs only ten of the twelve jurors to vote for a conviction or an acquittal.

in the second trial, we were able to secure a not guilty verdict by an 11 to 1 vote. The strategy remained the same, but something different happened in New Orleans. It concerned the jury selection and the use of drugs during the entire proceedings. Every night while in New Orleans, the defense attorney took pills, smoked marijuana, or snorted cocaine. The use of drugs was recreational, but used.

The Baton Rouge issue was very pervasive in this trial and often used by both the defense and prosecutor to secure the best jurors for either side. The *Louisiana Criminal Code of Procedure* allows for peremptory challenges for both parties. As such, either side can strike a potential juror for any reason except race. Yet, both the defense and the prosecution did it. It is based on the infamous Supreme Court case of Baston v. Kentucky. A defense attorney or prosecuting attorney cannot strike a prospective juror because of race; it must be done for a lawful cause. When the public cried for a second trial, we had to show a pattern of excluding jurors because of one's race, the strategy being that the defendant and the state are entitled to a jury of his peers.

> Should a lawyer strike a prospective juror simply because of the color of his or her skin?
>
> Should a lawyer deny striking a prospective juror because of his race when asked by the presiding judge?

Should a lawyer use drugs during any stage of trying a criminal case? If so, what recourse, if any, would the defendant have?

State of Louisiana
Versus
Naqill Ruffin:
The Killing of a Deputy Sheriff

The initial arrest and actual trial took approximately four months from start to finish. It was probably one of the saddest trials I was affiliated with during my seven years of practice. It concerned a drug bust that went sour. Newsflashes were everywhere: "A young deputy sheriff killed in the line of duty while trying to stop a federal agent from being killed."

The headlines range from one part of Baton Rouge to the south end of Louisiana to the north end of Louisiana. Captions were printed, and television coverage swelled every day for the next four months after his arrest.

Two Bank's residents (Bank's is a very low-income area in Baton Rouge) contacted Naquil Ruffin about a drug purchase and needed his muscle to carry it out. He would be paid $2,000 for his efforts. The US Postal Service was aware that of one of its employees was selling drugs to coworkers, and information was concealed until verified by someone who witnessed an actual sale on post office property. The ansaction gave the federal government jurisdiction in the matter. Later, an agent from the US Postal Service arrested the employee for selling contraband.

The employee agreed to act as an informant. The informant negotiated a drug deal with one of the Bank's residents to set up a buy at the Best Western Motel. The Postal Service contacted local authorities for assistance. They rented an adjoining room at the Best Western to monitor the transaction between the drug dealers and the informant. A postal agent agreed to assist and protect the informant by acting as his partner in the deal. The two Bank's residents never intended to purchase the drugs.

Naquil and the buyer went to the rented motel room, while the other Bank's residents waited outside with the car running for a quick getaway. The buyer asked to see the drugs, and the seller (informant) asked to see the buy money. Both were stalling. Suddenly, Naquil pulled a gun and requested the drugs. The postal agent tried to stall Naquil until he shouted, "Let's kill the motherfucker, and take the fucking drugs." Not wanting to take any chances or risks, and not knowing the informant's and undercover officer's immediate danger, the officers in the adjoining room decided to come to their aid.

Within seconds, the postal agents and local authorities, who were listening in the adjoining room, rushed the room by unlocking the door to the adjacent room.

Many events occurred during the melee. No one pers[on] knew what happened. When the smoke cleared, an officer lay wounded. "Why did you shoot me?" he asked. No one knew Naquil shot him. He was quickly taken to the hospital and was later pronounced dead. Naquil was arrested and charged with first-degree murder for killing the young deputy sheriff.

Naquil's family hired me to represent him in the matter. It was a formidable task. The city was in an uproar and demanded the death penalty for the triggerman responsible for the line-of-duty killing of a twenty-three-year-old deputy sheriff, Gerald Simons. Newspapers and television reports painted the officer as a courageous young man coming to the aid of a fellow officer in danger of losing his life during the drug transaction.

The intense media coverage created the felt need to rush to judgment. It was the first and only case in which the state and defense had to be ready for trial in four months. Judge L. J. Hymel did not grant any continuances and was adamant about trying Naquil on the scheduled date. We ran through the proceedings within two months.

The next month, I filed a change of venue, but it was ignored despite widespread media coverage. Judge Hymel was determined to keep this trial on course, regardless of whether Naquil's constitutional rights were being violated, especially considering pretrial publicity. The pretrial blicity in the Cynthia Porche and Henry Bennett trials were widespread. Naquil's case was no different from those cases, which were transferred to another parish because of publicity.

Jury selection took six weeks, and both sides were growing angrily tiresome of the task. The opening statement drew more than several hundred law enforcement officers from around the state to support one of their dead comrades. The courtroom's capacity was taxed, leaving standing room only with several hundred people struggling for positions in the courtroom. With each day's passing, the media sensationalized the entire proceedings.

One of the most gruesome presentations by a prosecuting attorney was showing the entrance and exit wounds of the slain officer and a recapitulation of the facts leading to his death. There were no dry eyes, including mine, as media representatives rushed to their respective offices to print or televise the drama of that day.

There was more drama the next day. The slain officer's family burst into whimpering cries until they could no longer hold back their shouts and tears. The judge jumped to his feet. The defense jumped to object about the emotional outburst by Officer Simons's immediate family. "Bailiffs, take the jury to the jury room, and the court stands adjourned," ordered Judge Hymel. "But I need to talk with the family members." After he spoke with the family, I continued to object to the family's emotional outbursts. The judge denied my motion for a mistrial, but I was allowed to note my objection for the record. It was to preserve any error for any appeals court to review. Failure to do so does not allow an appeals court to view any errors made by the court, defense attorney, or prosecutor. A significant error could result in the overturning of a guilty verdict.

The jury returned, and the prosecutor continued to hammer the defendant as a sleazy, low-life scum of the earth for killing this promising and dedicated officer who put fellow officers' lives before his own. He painted a picture that evoked the only way to vindicate his death was to convict Naquil of first-degree murder. The state rested.

We did not question many of the state's witnesses other than to establish that Naquil was not the person who fired the shot that killed Officer Simons. The ballistic expert we employed indicated that the flight of the bullet could not have come from the direction where Naquil stood. It had to come from the direction of the informant or the undercover agent.

Moreover, the pathologist also indicated that the bullet's flight could not have come from a standing position. It had to come from someone sitting. And Naquil was too close to the victim for him to not have stippling around the entrance wound. However, both experts refused to testify because of their past affiliations within their respective professions.

ne was an ex-police officer, and the other trained the pathologist who was testifying for the state. Of course, this was problematic when I learned that information.

On direct examination, I had to establish that the undercover agent had a pistol strapped to his leg. As he discussed the sale of cocaine, Naquil's attention was diverted, and the agent eased his pants leg up to where his gun was in a ready stance. When the officers in the adjoining room burst through the door, Naquil's attention was distracted, so the officer had ample time to pull his revolver and shoot in Naquil's direction. Unfortunately, Officer Simons ran in front of Naquil and was shot instead.

Officer Felton Clark testified that all revolvers used during a killing had to be turned into internal affairs to be inspected. The officer further testified that the only pistol not turned in was the undercover agent's gun. The agent testified he cleaned his revolver after the crime and did not turn his gun into internal affairs. He testified that he did get a shot off in Naquil's direction, which could have killed Officer Simons. But there was no way of knowing without the testimony of my expert witness.

Even though I wanted to pursue this line of questioning, I knew it would be futile because the defendant does not have to fire the gun to be tried as a principal to first-degree murder. To pursue this line of questioning would only injure both officers, who had enough to deal with concerning the death of a fallen officer. The officers were honest people who would have testified if called to do so. The testimony would have injured their relationships with fellow officers. I did not want to damage that because the jury was going to convict Naquil anyway.

I left them alone, knowing that I could have created reasonable doubt. It really would not have mattered with this jury, which incidentally was all white. One juror was an African American who pretended to be white; being African Americans, we could tell. I knew going in I had lost that juror because he had identity issues and would go into the jury room proving that he belonged. Should I have exposed him to his race?

The jury found Naquil guilty of first-degree murder. The next phase was the penalty; the prosecutor was seeking death. It was one of the most emotional occurrences I ever witnessed. Every possible emotion was dripping from my breast. I was physically and emotionally drained.

I had to muster enough strength to continue with the penalty phase of the trial. I finally knew what it was like to have a person's life in your hands. Mike Erwin was his usual dynamic self. In his closing statement, he said, "I, Gerald Simons, do hereby pledge that I will uphold the laws and the constitution of Louisiana and the United States of America. He cannot do that anymore." Tears flowed from his eyes as he placed the oath of office form on the table and walked away, tears dropping on to the prosecutor's table.

As he sat, I wanted to go over to his table and kick him in his legs. He was excellent. I tried to remind each juror of the oaths they made to Naquil as I explained what happened on that black day in Baton Rouge. I used every conceivable reason as to why they should not execute him. I felt I was equally as compelling as Mike. The jury was deadlocked. The judge dismissed the jury and immediately imposed the life sentence.

> Should a lawyer pursue a line of questioning he or she knows will lead to incriminating evidence that will not exonerate the client but cause injury to innocent persons?

> Should a lawyer declare his or her experts hostile and, as such, have the judge compel them to testify?

> Should a lawyer take an unpopular case despite undue influence by members of his or her family and friends?

> Should a lawyer ask the court to take judicial notice of the law enforcement officers attending the trial as a form of subtle intimidation when he or she knows repercussions may derive therefrom?

CHAPTER 9

Personal Convictions

United States of America
Versus
Orscini L. Beard

The adage, "You live by the sword, you'll die by the sword," certainly applies to me. After defending so many criminal cases and being successful in the process, I found myself in the courtroom charged with bankruptcy fraud in not declaring a $175,000 attorney's fee received from the state for my successful defense of Cynthia Porche on the charge of malfeasance in office.

The state of Louisiana had to reimburse Cynthia's legal expense after she was found not guilty by a jury. Under a state statute, if a public or civil servant is charged with a crime in the performance of his or her duty on behalf of the state, the individual is entitled to reimbursement of any legal expenses incurred if a jury or judge has vindicated the person in a court of competent jurisdiction. This case caused one of many events in my life. It was similar to the boomerang theory. You cast it out, and it returns to you.

Since a jury had found Cynthia not guilty, she was entitled to submit an itemized invoice for reimbursement of legal expenses. As I represented her, I introduced a detailed bill of work to the legislature in the form of a house-bill. The bill must be endorsed by a state representative for it to move from the House to the Senate. If not, the bill can lie dormant for a long time.

It was at this time that I had filed a chapter 13 in the US Bankruptcy Court. Chapter 13 allows a debtor to reorganize indebtedness by paying a fraction of what is owed to creditors until the bankruptcy judge approves such a plan. There are several hearings before being declared bankrupt. At one point, the judge ruled that I had a workable plan. But he retired from the bench before signing his name to the plan.

The creditors used this opportunity to advance their disdain for the plan. When a visiting bankruptcy judge from Shreveport finished the proceedings, the creditors urged reconsideration. The visiting bankruptcy judge held a hearing from Shreveport. He struggled over more than a thousand pages of documents and testimony from prior hearings before deciding to convert me to a chapter 7 bankruptcy. For my life, I could not understand how he could circumvent a previous ruling made by the retiring bankruptcy judge. He had studied my case from the initial filing up to and including the first judge's decision on the matter. When did he have the opportunity to study—or

Many of her questions focused on the whereabouts of that $175,000. I refused to answer those questions because the attorney's fees should not have been discussed during the 331 hearing as they were not included as a part of the bankruptcy. I did testify that the $175,000 was intact. The trustee repeatedly asked that I reconsider my decision to cooperate, but I steadfastly refused to do so. The meeting was adjourned.

At this juncture, it is interesting to note that the $175,000 was common knowledge to the city of Baton Rouge. It was also common knowledge that a state representative was assisting me in my endeavors to have the state pay me for representing Cynthia. What was not known was that there was an undisclosed agreement the representative and I that he receive 10 percent of the attorney's fees paid by the state. If I had not secured his support or his endorsement of the bill, the matter would have taken a very long time getting through the legislature. Given my financial situation, I could not afford to allow the bill to lie dormant until the legislators decided to act on my request for reimbursement in the not so distant future. Therefore, I had to deal with this state representative. Incidentally, he is also a licensed attorney.

Had I not received the attorney's fee, my financial empire could be ruin. My law practice was thriving, but two of my business ventures were having cash-flow problems. I had invested in Denaté, an exclusive exotic shoe store, that started showing signs of improvement, but I needed cash to stay afloat. Although my outside business ventures were struggling, and I was perplexed, I knew if I could get my hands on the $175,000, all my financial woes would be over. Nothing was farther from the truth. My troubles were just beginning.

The next day, I received a subpoena from the US District Court to appear in open court at 3:00 p.m. I had to bring any documents or legal precedents to show cause why the $175,000 in attorney's fees received from the state should not be included in the bankruptcy proceedings. Ordinarily, Judge Louis Phillips, who had been recently appointed for the Middle District Bankruptcy Court, would have heard the matter, but he was out of town. Therefore, Judge Polozola issued the subpoena.

My attorney and I appeared with our documents, but the court quickly held me in contempt for refusing to cooperate. Several times, my attorney advised me to turn over my assets to the trustee. Still, the entire amount was not intact after testifying in the US District Court otherwise. How desperately I wanted to tell the court. Yet, I could not. I had already given State Representative Charles Jones $25,000 in cash for assisting me in recovering my expenses for representing Cynthia. Before giving Charles the money, I had consulted two local attorneys, and both concurred that I should give him the money and put the whole ordeal behind me. I told them that I was in a bankruptcy and knew it might present problems with the trustee. I also conveyed that thought to Charles, but he was so eager to receive the money that nothing else mattered. I was also aware that it was against the law to give a public official something of value to derive a favor thereof when it was his elected duty to do so. These perplexing problems were running in and out of my subconscious as Judge Polozoa asked that I reconsider my decision to tell the court the whereabouts of the $175,000 attorney's fees. Again, I refused to do so, knowing that I would be incarcerated within minutes. But it would give me ample time to gather my thoughts. As I was led away in handcuffs, the judge imposed a fine of $10,000 a day, and each day I refused to purge myself, the fine accelerated to $20,000. The next day, the penalty would be doubled to $40,000, and so on. I knew it was not going to take too long for the $175,000 to dissipate.

I was brought back into court to purge myself the next day. Consequently, I did more harm than I had done the day before and damaged any chance of escaping legal ramifications. I made several misleading statements about what happened to some of the money. But I eventually told the court what banks and what people were in possession of the remaining portion of the $175,000. From my calculation, approximately $110,000, real and personal property, valued at more than a million dollars, were retrieved by the court and handed over to the trustee for supervision. With the infusion of money, my estate was valued at almost a million dollars. Ironically, my indebtedness was less than what I owed to the creditors.

It was during this hearing that my actual troubles surfaced. Because I made several misleading or erroneous statements both in the 331 meetings and in federal court, the US Attorney General's office was instructed to investigate my misdoings. On the ninth day of October 1989, a federal grand jury indicted me on several counts of perjury.

I hired the best criminal attorney in the United States in general and in Louisiana particularly. Since I was destitute, I could not afford to pay him for his service. Alcide Gray was more than willing to represent me regardless of my financial condition. Although I had several other prominent and qualified attorneys willing to represent me for no fee, I declined their services because their motives were not sincere. Al was diligent and tenacious and initially lacking in integrity. He was a very close friend of Charles Jones and kept him apprised of what was going on in my case. On several occasions, I was informed that he told Charles and others how I was snitching on everyone. Al did not know that I knew how the US attorney felt about me, and I also knew how to manipulate the system.

I did not want to testify against anyone. It was necessary to persuade them to believe I was not a credible witness. This, of course, stopped them from granting me immunity from prosecution. I had to make them think that I was incapable of telling the truth about anything so they would leave me alone. My attorney and others concerned about the outcome of the trial also called my demeanor into question. They did not know what to expect if I took the stand to testify against Charles. What would I do? This question was probably asked many times by US Attorney Ray Lamonica.

I knew how desperately they wanted Charles Jones and others, and I was not going to let them use me to get him. My family was suffering enough from my stupidity. So I pleaded to one count of bankruptcy fraud, which carries a maximum penalty of fourteen months. But the court erroneously interpreted the statute as to what is perjury per se, or what is bankruptcy fraud under the present law. This is to say, perjury under the new sentencing guidelines increases the punishment to a maximum of twenty-seven months instead of fourteen months for bankruptcy fraud.

The US Probation Office conducted a presentence investigation, which was submitted to Judge Donovon Parker. Judge Parker sentenced me at the top of the sentencing guideline because I was an attorney. I did not receive a two-point deduction because I did not accept responsibility for my actions. The week before I was sentenced, the same judge sentenced another lawyer, who was much more seasoned than I, to one year and a day. The significance of the one day means that he has to serve four months of his sentence under the old sentencing guidelines. Had he been sentenced under the new guidelines, he would have received an actual sentence of six months of incarceration. That extra day allows him to be released from federal custody within four months of incarceration. This attorney was responsible for citizens of Louisiana losing their life savings in what was called the "La Reel scandal." He was not ordered to pay for the time he was incarcerated, as I was ordered to do. On the other hand, my crime involved only my family and me. I am not trying to cast any aspersions about the attorney. I am only drawing a parallel to my particular case.

I had until 1:00 p.m. on the fifth of December to surrender to the Bureau Prison in Texarkana, Texas. I had two months to get my affairs in order. What was I to do? My caseload was overwhelming, and I had to do something. I spoke with several attorneys about handling some of my cases. But what about the two matters scheduled for trial in November. What was I to do? I was confused, and I knew I had to do something. I had started using drugs and became obsessed with it. I was addicted but refused to acknowledge my actions. I smoked and snorted cocaine liked there was no tomorrow. I was determined to finish my two trials, so I put away the drugs and prepared for the trials.

Then I discovered the Feds were not through with me yet. I tried to get my affairs in order, but they subpoenaed me to appear before a grand jury to testify about the facts and circumstances surrounding an alleged payoff to Representative Charles Jones. They wanted me to tell what I knew about paying him to assist me in my efforts to have Cynthia's attorney fees paid.

Several times Al wanted to withdraw as my attorney because of his relationship with Charles. When he realized his relationship with Charles was influencing his decision to represent me, he realized it was impossible to represent my best interests. But he did a fantastic job in representing me. Since I had already pleaded, I could no longer avail myself of the Fifth Amendment. Still, I refused to testify on the grounds it might tend to incriminate me and to testify truthfully about the facts and circumstances surrounding this crime.

I was in a box and did not know it. I had anticipated being called me before the grand jury after I pleaded. Ray, who was prosecuting, was playing chess, and he had just said, "Checkmate." If I refused, Ray would bring me before a judge and explain that I refused to testify. As a result, the judge could hold me in contempt, which can last as long as eighteen months, the length of the grand jury's session. Once the grand jury's term expires, another grand jury would be called, and I could again be brought before it to testify. And If I refused, the same process could be repeated.

I was stripped of any protection under the US Constitution. And I knew what to do in the grand jury room. I was enraged. I cursed Ray and others for bringing me before them. I said that all I wanted to do was to do my time for the crime, and I was responsible for my demise. Ray was so frustrated, he left me alone. I called it a checkmate because I had to be deemed a believable witness. And I had proven I would be neither believable nor reliable.

Should a lawyer reframe from even the slightest signs of impropriety?

Should a lawyer tell the truth about the facts and circumstances he or she was involved in when ordered by the court to do so?

Should a lawyer enter into a deal with another lawyer to secure funds from the state that are lawfully his or hers, but to achieve them expediently, the other party needs a fee to do so?

Should a lawyer represent a client when he or she knows from the beginning it might cause a conflict of interest?

Should a lawyer tell the client to lie or refuse to testify before a grand jury when the lawyer knows it will affect the client's position with the law?

Should a lawyer refuse to assist or turn over disputed funds to the trustee when ordered to do so?

Should a lawyer refuse to obey a court order to turn over funds from a pending case when he or she knows that the money could part of a bankruptcy filing?

Should a lawyer refuse to cooperate with a trustee or federal judge?

Should a lawyer refuse to cooperate with a federal grand jury when he would violate his moral conviction by being a snitch?

Should a lawyer reveal to the proper authority any illegal activity of a public official when he or she knows it is against the law to pay the public official a fee for doing what he or she was elected to do?

Should a lawyer represent a client when he or she knows the extent of the criminal investigation of a personal friend by his or her representation of the client?

Should a lawyer use personal position to gain information about a friend's involvement in the crime when representing one of the parties?

Should a lawyer use his or her position to assist a friend's possible defense if it occurs in the event?

State of Louisiana
Versus
James Williams

Although I stood as a convicted felon whose incarceration was within a month away, I still had an obligation to fulfill my commitments to my clients. The Louisiana Bar Association frowns on any lawyers who do not fulfill their obligations to their clients. I had to resolve as many cases as possible before leaving for prison. If I were to have any chance whatsoever of regaining my license to practice, it was necessary to ask other lawyers to handle some of my cases. I managed to handle a few cases before leaving for prison. Two trials were pending from previous pretrial matters that had to be resolved before leaving for prison.

I could not trust my colleagues to handle these particular matters because of such short notice and the complexity of the trials. Further, the clients still believed I would represent them vigorously and diligently, regardless of my current situation. I repeatedly asked my clients whether they wanted someone else to represent them since I had my problems, but they vehemently declined my offer. I offered to reimburse them, but they refused.

James Williams came to the house to discuss the merits of the case since the law office would be soon closing. He even picked me up for all scheduled court appearances or any other matters about his case.

On several occasions, Assistant District Attorney Jessie Mean and I discussed a possible plea, but the discussion broke down due in part to the length of sentence involved if James pleaded to bribing a juror. The deal was a token. A juror alleged that James tried to give her money if she found his wife not guilty on the charge of theft. His wife was found guilty of felony theft. And shortly after that, James was indicted and charged with bribery.

The trial was held in a tiny and close-knit community where everyone knew each other. The city was divided about the case. There were severe racial overtones. The entire community was aware of this case and horrified that one of its citizens could have been stupid enough to bribe another of its citizens.

The integrity of the jury system and the community was on trial. I had to convince prospective jurors not to make up their minds until they heard all the evidence. Moreover, I had to convince them that it was his word against hers. I told the story of two children who blamed each other for a broken lamp. One cried, "He did it, Mommy," while the other cried, "He did it, Mommy." Whom do you believe when you were not present? Both of them were claiming to be innocent. A true mother's dilemma.

I had to select jurors who were rearing more than one child and had experienced this dilemma. It was a phenomenal task, but like all trial attorneys who love being in a court of drama, I rose to the occasion. My problems were out of the moment; the only thing on my mind was the trial at hand and how to obtain a not guilty verdict for my client.

After several days of selecting a jury and hearing the witnesses' testimonies, the jury could not render a verdict. It was a hung jury. The jury could not determine whether my client or the prosecution's key witness was telling the truth. I created reasonable doubt in the minds of the jury. I knew the defendant attempted to bribe the key witness, but I told him to stop telling me he did. His testimony proved to be the critical factor in hanging the jury.

The district attorney decided not to retry James, and he was released from any further prosecution by the state of Louisiana.

> Should a lawyer try a case when facing a prison term?

> Should a lawyer fulfill his or her obligation despite the Bar Association's attitude about finishing your obligation to your client when personal problems may tend to cloud his or her legal and moral judgment?

Should an attorney decline to represent a client even though the client wants that particular attorney?

Should a lawyer put the client on the stand when he or she knows the client may mislead the jury during questioning?

State of Louisiana
Versus
Donald Melancon

The pressure of finishing a trial and starting another trial within weeks of each other was beginning to tax me emotionally and physically. But I was determined to fulfill my client obligations before departing for prison. The atmosphere was suffocating me. I had been subpoenaed to appear in federal court to testify before a grand jury in Baton Rouge, and at the same time and day, I was also subpoenaed to appear in criminal court in Vidalia, Louisiana, for a motion hearing and eventual trial. What was I to do?

My conviction for trying cases was more substantial than my legal obligation to appear in federal court. I wanted to finish this case, and I didn't want to reschedule it. I knew if I did, it would present a problem for both my client and me. I also knew the judge wanted to resolve this matter without further delays. The judge was receiving pressure from the citizens because of the publicity this case had generated. And to some degree, there was an implication in the newspaper article that I was involved in the drug deal with two undercover agents since my wife owned the van, and her first cousin was arrested driving the van. The innuendos were made by the media. The pressure from the media called for an immediate trial.

Going in, I knew there would be no delay. So I called Judge Gremillion and explained my dilemma to him. He told me to come to Vidalia, and he would sort things out. He called the US Attorney's office to explain my situation to them. However, they wanted me back in Baton Rouge right now! If I did not return within the hour, they would have federal marshals escort me back to Baton Rouge in handcuffs. The judge barked at the threat and admonished them for intimidating him because they were the Feds. "It is commendable that this young attorney is trying to fulfill his obligation when he leaves for prison within weeks. I don't know many other lawyers who would have done the same," explained the judge. "I will not allow him to be taken from this court in handcuffs when he is only trying to do his job for his client. I'll inform the media and other people how you have tried to use your power to force him to appear in your court, thereby showing your disdain for the power of the state court."

I was certainly glad that he called Ray. I knew if I had tried to explain my situation, given my current status with them, Ray would have gotten the judge to postpone the trial, or he would have called a federal judge to issue a warrant for my arrest and stop me from appearing in court to represent Donald. The District Attorney's office also called the US Attorney's office to voice their displeasure over the exertion of undue pressure to compel me to appear before the grand jury instead of representing my client. The US Attorney acquiesced.

Donald was charged with two counts of selling a dangerous substance to two undercover agents; they were from different parishes. The agents were used in this parish because their identities were unknown to the drug dealers. To prevent the influx of drugs into the tri-city area, a task force had been created. Police officers and deputy sheriffs from other parishes acted as undercover agents.

One of the agents, who was from Ferriday, alleged that he purchased a $20 piece of crack cocaine from Donald on two occasions. He also testified that he did not know Donald before the sale, and the entire transaction took approximately five to ten seconds, at best. Further, he testified that it was a very dark night with little or no illumination. When asked, "How were you able to recognize Donald since you did not know him before the transaction?" he responded by saying, "Deputy David Cowen showed me a picture of him after the drug buy."

When I then asked, "Have he seen him since the transaction?" he replied no. It had been almost a year before he was tried for the crime. "Had you been given a picture of Donald before testifying?" Again he answered no. I turned his attention to the description of Donald in the police report, which he had written. The description depicted a short, dark-complected man with a close haircut. I asked Donald to stand, while the officer explained the discrepancy in this description of Donald. Donald was tall, had a fair complexion, was thin, and had a Jheri curl. I also called his attention to his testimony at the preliminary examination, in which he described Donald and the particular time of night of the alleged drug transaction. Again it was distorted.

The officers' testimonies were more of the same with many discrepancies. Donald needed to take the stand in to refute the undercover officers' damaging testimony. I confronted him about the prospect of misleading the jury by his testimony since I was aware he had sold to both agents. They were banking on the defendant's misidentification because without identification, one of the elements required to convict him was absent. I knew I could play the identification card with the jury. But I did not want to present Donald as an innocent victim who was being picked on by local authorities because of his prior conviction. I had to be very careful not to overdo it.

Donald's testimony was very misleading in explaining the critical statements made by the witnesses. Some witnesses wanted to testify that he was with them when the alleged drug transaction transpired. Should I allow these witnesses to testify on his behalf when I knew that the alibi was bogus? The witnesses testified, and the jury voted 8 to 4 in favor of acquitting him.

In my closing argument, I zeroed in on the misidentification by repeating my question, "How can you …" I reiterated that, echoing how could he remember the defendant now when he hadn't seen him in over ten months? The alleged drug transaction took only five to ten seconds to complete on a very dark night, and the officers had not known the defendant before the alleged drug transaction. The testimony of Deputy Cowen verified the allegations.

I also argued the alibi theory to the jury. The jury was deadlocked, and the judge declared a mistrial. Note: I have more information about identification.

> Should a lawyer fulfill his or her obligation to a client despite a federal grand jury subpoena?
>
> Should a lawyer be forced to try a case when considering his or her situation?
>
> Should a lawyer try a case considering his or her emotional and physical states of mind?
>
> Should a US Attorney force a lawyer to appear before a grand jury when he or she

knows about a pending trial before issuing the subpoena but has the subpoena issued anyway?

Should a judge intervene in a federal matter when there is sufficient or just cause to do so?

Should the district attorney intervene in a federal matter as an attorney for a cause?

Should a US Attorney use his or her office to force an attorney to appear before a grand jury when he or she knows the attorney has a trial on the same day as the grand jury appearance?

Should a lawyer allow the client to take the stand to testify when he or she knows the client will give misleading testimony?

Should a lawyer allow witnesses to take the stand to testify when he or she knows the witness will give misleading testimony?

Should a lawyer argue in the closing about identification and alibi when he or she knows the client sold drugs to the undercover agents?

Should a lawyer represent a client when there is an implication of his or her involvement with the client's illegal transaction?

State of Louisiana
Versus
Kevin Mosley

This case was dumped into my lap. The defendant was found guilty of armed robbery. Brady Jones, who was a public defender, tried the case. The defendant was a two-time loser, and the district attorney's office intended to file a "habitual offender" motion. A friend of a friend asked me if I could assist the defendant. I did not want to take on another case, given my current situation. The defendant was compelling about his innocence, so I ventured into muddy waters when I knew I already had too much on my plate,

I outlined my plan of attack in appealing issues of errors. I was not hired to represent him for any other pending matters, including the habitual offender motion, but somehow my motion to enroll and substitute counsel was interpreted prematurely by the court. Brady was delighted to withdraw from the case, and I wanted to find out why.

Preparing for the habitual offender motion was counterproductive. The preparation disrupted my timetable tremendously in terms of his appeal. I had only a few days remaining before turning myself in to the Bureau of Prisons in Texarkana. As such, I had one more trial to prepare.

I was not successful in defeating the motion because there was not a point of clarity on the statute as to when the clock ticks as the release date from prison or custody of probation and parole to invoke the habitual offender act. Of course, I assigned an error to the judge's ruling, but this did not sit well with my client. He was growing dissatisfied with me and how he was being represented. I candidly pointed out that I was not hired to represent him on the motion, but I, nevertheless, did so as a matter of comity to advance his cause.

After the hearing, Judge Michael McDonald set a sentencing hearing for the next week. Again I had to prepare for the sentencing hearing. Many lawyers feel that sentencing hearings are merely perfunctory, at best. But I prepared for sentencing hearings; I do not see them as meager tasks. I subpoenaed witnesses to testify on behalf of my client and researched the habitual offender law to argue for reconsideration before sentencing. The judge took my argument under advisement.

The judge ruled that my argument had merit and reduced his initial sentence from twenty-five to fourteen years at hard labor with the Department of Corrections. The judge set return dates for his appeal. I was unsure whether I would be able to meet those return days, especially since I would be trying a significant drug case in his courtroom within the next two weeks.

The preparation for the next trial and the appeal was overwhelming. I could not meet both obligations competently, and I expressed my dilemma to Judge McDonald during ex parte hearing. "I don't want to infringe or jeopardize any of my client's constitutional rights because of my lack of diligence," I said out of an abundance of caution. He immediately relieved me from the Mosley case but refused to do so for the Hendricks brothers' case. I had to get the same clearance from Judge Hester in the case.

My client was very disgruntled about the sentence and my withdrawal. Every opportunity he had to express his dismay, he took advantage of by sending me threatening letters before and after my incarceration. He even took out a contract on my life but was unsuccessful in accomplishing his feat because of my good will in the criminal community.

> Should a lawyer accept another client given his or current status with the Louisiana Bar Association and future prison date?
>
> Should a lawyer immediately inform a judge about conflicting return dates for an appeal when he or she becomes aware of the dates?

Should a lawyer continue to represent a disgusted client when he or she knows about his dangerous propensities?

Should a lawyer notify the proper authorities when he or she receives threatening letters from a former client?

Should a lawyer notify a judge about a client's cause when he or she can no longer pursue that cause diligently?

State of Louisiana
Versus
the Hendrick Brothers

Should a lawyer pursue a client's cause when he or she has only a few weeks before entering prison? Should a lawyer fulfill his or her obligation to a client because it will be looked upon favorably by the Louisiana Bar Association when he or she files for readmittance? Those are questions I considered with this case.

Of all my cases, this one has plagued me more than any case I have ever tried, even today. I was successful in having charges dropped against the youngest member of the family but was depressed by the other brothers' outcome.

The brothers are from a single-parent home. The mother worked for many years as a housekeeper-maid for a wealthy family from Miami. She saved every penny she could get her hands on for their education. One of the brothers was a talented football player for Southern University with aspirations of playing professional football, but he injured his knee. He was making a comeback while working out with a local team in Miami. The middle son was probably the most intelligent and arrogant of the brothers.

The mother asked the oldest brother to accompany the middle and youngest brothers to Baton Rouge. He did not want to travel to Baton Rouge but did so because of his love for his mother. Granted, he was aware of his middle brother's plan to purchase a kilogram of cocaine before departing for Baton Rouge. Their mother had given them her life savings in the pursuit of academic excellence at Southern University. They decided to double their mother's investment by purchasing the cocaine from a neighborhood friend. The mother was investing in their future, but they took her life savings and invested them in drugs to double the dividends.

An informant identified the seller and house in which he had made several controlled buys. A controlled buy is when an informant is patted down for any other drugs or money in his possession before entering the targeted house. The local authorities observe the house's front and back. After the purchase is made, he is patted again for any drugs or money. He is taken into custody while the local authorities continue to watch the resident for the traffic of potential drug addicts. Law enforcement takes this information to the judge for a search warrant. A search warrant was executed on the premises while the brothers and their girlfriends were asleep. The search revealed a half-kilo of cocaine. The brothers were arrested for possession of a known dangerous substance, commonly known as cocaine, with the intent to distribute.

I filed the various motions, including a motion to suppress. But Judge McDonald ruled against us, and a trial date was set. "There will be no postponement in this trial," declared the judge. This case was tried quicker than the Naquil Ruffin case.

The arresting officers contacted another attorney to assist the brothers in their endeavor, but their sister was not pleased with the attorney's demeanor or intelligence. He advised the brothers to cooperate with the authorities to receive a favorable sentencing recommendation to the district attorney and judge. An officer later contacted me and asked if my clients would cooperate in apprehending a significant figure in the drug trafficking trade. If so, it would look good with the judge when they were sentenced. But had they cooperated, the defendants would have jeopardized their entire family.

On several occasions, Assistant District Attorney Robert Peridiant offered a five-year sentence or to leave sentencing to the judge with the understanding the younger brother would not be prosecuted. But I wanted a probated sentence for the other two brothers.

The assistant district attorney refused my counteroffer. "If convicted, each of you will be exposed to five to thirty years with or without hard labor because of the quantity of cocaine found in your possession," I explained to them. They were adamant in their conviction of trying the case, even in the face of my judgment. The mother, who was unaware of the truth of the matter believed in her sons' innocence and expressed the desire to try the case. At one point, I had to force the brothers to tell their mother the truth about their involvement in the scheme of things, but I was met with opposition for a long time, which interfered with the preparation for trial.

Eventually, the brothers confided in the mother and asked me to do what I could for them. I again requested a deal from the assistant district attorney, but he would not budge from his initial offer, other than saying he might consider probation for the oldest brother, but the middle brother had to do some form of incarceration. I contacted a pretrial expert who had the ear of Judge McDonald to intercede on my clients' behalf, but the judge definitely wanted him to do some time in prison. To what extent, I did not know as he would not commit himself. I was dubious about having my clients stand bare-naked before the judge without some form of commitment to the length of the sentence that might be imposed.

It is particularly true when considering the *State* of Louisiana v. Paul Williams, who was charged with five counts of attempted first-degree murder. Paul was an irate boyfriend whose girlfriend used him financially. He decided to revenge this misdeed by raiding his girlfriend's home. He fired shots at all the occupants, seriously wounding and injuring two of her family members. There were little children in the house. Judge Bob Hester was willing to accept a plea in the matter, and the assistant district attorney left the matter up to the judge. The judge ordered a presentence investigation but would not commit himself to the length of the sentence. He did intimate a cap of ten years to run consecutively to two charges and the other to run concurrently.

A presentence investigation was filed with the court. I was given an opportunity to review the report and reschedule a sentencing hearing. I subpoenaed witnesses but knew going into the hearing that the judge would not abide by his initial commitment. As I suspected, he gave Paul one hundred years, all running consecutively. "I know this is a lengthy sentence, and it is the only one I can justify in my mind considering the gravity of the crime. If your client is to have any redress, it will be with the First Circuit Court of Appeals on the grounds of an excessive sentence," said Judge Hester.

It was a double-edged sword, one I have held many times in the sentencing of clients. Judge Hester's statement surfaced in the Hendricks case. I did not want to see this child in prison with a lengthy sentence when I knew deep down he had just made a grave mistake, although he has not shown remorse for his involvement in the crime. Judge McDonald felt the same about the middle brother because of his previous courtroom demeanor. I was afraid he would consider this in sentencing him if he decided to plead.

Time was seriously against me; I was within a week of my incarceration. What was I to do? Should I force him to plead, or should I go to trial, knowing what the judge might do if my clients were convicted of the charges? My impending imprisonment and financial woes compounded all of this. I asked myself, "Am I my brother's keeper?"

If ever an adage applied, my brother's keeper was in full force in this case. Both the assistant district attorney and judge looked upon the older brother favorably. I knew he could have been probated, but he was unwilling to plead if his brother received a lengthy sentence. At this point, I should have filed a motion to withdraw from representing the older brother, but I did not. I did, however, file a motion for severance, but it was denied. I did assign error to the judge's ruling, which was later overturned by the First Circuit Court of Appeals.

The trial lasted a week, and the jury found both brothers guilty as charged. The judge remanded both to the parish prison pending sentencing. A presentence investigation was ordered, but the judge refused to allow them to continue on bond. The commotion in the courtroom was breathtaking as family members and defendants cried as the bailiff led the brothers off to jail. When I realized I had failed them, tears poured from my eyes. It was certainly not my best performance in the courtroom. I did not do my typical job. I worked hard to prepare for the trial, but there were occasional bouts of drug use and drinking.

> Should a lawyer refrain from representing a codefendant when his or her defense is antagonistic to the other defendant(s)?

> Should a lawyer inform the client's mother of the truth of the case when doing so might breach attorney-client privilege?

> Should a lawyer represent a client or clients given the circumstances of his or her pending incarceration?

> Should a lawyer admit drug involvement to his or her client or the Louisiana Bar Association during the preparation of a trial?

> Should an attorney be involved with local authorities to receive a favorable sentencing recommendation for his or her clients?

Should an attorney allow a client to cooperate when doing so may jeopardize the client's entire family?

Should an attorney accept a call from local authorities to represent clients they arrested to gain an advantage with the clients?

Although I informed my prospective clients of my impending incarceration, there were several incidents in which attorney's fees were accepted.

A case in point was the appeal of a convicted murder in Amite, Louisiana. The mother paid me to complete his appeal. I worked ardently on the appeal but ran out of time. An associate agreed to finish what I started but requested additional funds from the mother. It is also true of a sister who paid me for handling a drug case in Plaquemine, Louisiana. The same attorney agreed to handle the case, but behind my back, he again requested additional monies to represent the client. You may think this is atypical of lawyers and that this might be an isolated incident. Or you may think that I have surrounded myself with unethical lawyers. But nothing is further from the truth. Many practicing attorneys have done similar acts in one form or another, and they don't think their actions are unethical. These cases were filed with the disciplinary board.

Should a lawyer agree to handle a matter on a pro bono basis but later request funds from the client or family members to do so?

Should a lawyer accept attorney's fees even though he informs his prospective clients of an indeterminate prison sentence?

Should a lawyer accept a case knowing he or she may be incarcerated before the completion of the case?

Printed in the United States
by Baker & Taylor Publisher Services